Kejom (Babanki) Linguistic Practices in Farming Economies

Pius W. Akumbu
Cornelius W. Wuchu

MAP
Kansas City (MO), USA

Kejom (Babanki) Linguistic Practices in Farming Economies

Pius W. Akumbu & Cornelius W. Wuchu

First Published in 2015

Miraclaire Academic Publications (MAP)
Kansas City, MO 64133, USA
www.miraclairepublishing.com / info@miraclairepublishing.com

In association with
Ken Scholars Publishing, Raytown, USA

Copyright © 2015 by MAP

ISBN-13: 978-0692475430
ISBN-10: 0692475435

All rights reserved
No part of this book may be reproduced, stored in a retrieval system, or transmitted, in any form or by any means, electronic, mechanical, photocopying, recording or otherwise, without the prior permission of the copyright owner.

Printed in the United States of America

Miraclaire Publishing makes every effort to ensure the accuracy of all the information ("Content") in its publications. However, Miraclaire and its agents and licensors make no representations or warranties whatsoever as to the accuracy, completeness, or suitability for any purpose of the Content and disclaim all such representations and warranties, whether expressed or implied to the maximum extent permitted by law. Any views expressed in this publication are the views of the author and are not necessarily the views of Miraclaire.

Table of Contents

List of Figures..v
List of Tables..v
Photos..v
Plates...vi
Preface...vii

Chapter One: General Introduction..........................1
1.0 Introduction..1
1.1 Geo-Historical Situation of Kejom Ketinguh.......1
1.2 Origin of Kejom Farmers..................................4
1.3 Linguistic Situation..8
1.4 Literature Review 10
1.4.1 Language..10
1.4.2 Agriculture..13
1.4.3 Culture...14
1.5 Motivation...15
1.6 Aims and Rationale 15
1.7 Layout of the Work..16

Chapter Two: Agricultural Productivity...................17
2.0 Introduction..17
2.1 Physical or Natural Factors............................17
2.1.1 Favourable Climatic Conditions..................17
2.1.2 Topography or Relief..................................19
2.1.3 Suitable Soil Conditions..............................22
2.1.4 Suitable Vegetation....................................24
2.2 Human and Economic Factors........................24
2.2.1 The Role of Research Centres and NGOs.....24
2.2.1.1 Livelihood NGO.......................................25
2.2.1.2 Cercle International Pour la Production et de la
         Création (CIPCRE).....................................25
2.2.1.3 Helvetas Cameroon..................................25

i

2.2.1.4 Heifer Project International (H.P.I)...........26
2.2.1.5 Other NGOs 26
2.2.2 Available Markets..............................26
2.2.3 Road Infrastructure............................29
2.3 Conclusion......................................30

Chapter Three: General Life of Farmers.............31
3.0 Introduction....................................31
3.1 Rituals Leading to the Planting Season..........31
3.1.1 *Bvàʔɔ̀ Tɔ̀fám* 'shrine sacrifice'.............32
3.1.2 *Mɔ̀ʔɔ̀ Vɔ̀nyìŋgɔ̀ŋ* 'sacrificing to the gods......32
3.2 Protection of Farms by the Population..........34
3.2.1 Protection from Witchcraft and Evil Spirits...35
3.2.2 Protection from Wild Animals and Birds........36
3.2.3 Protection from Thieves.......................36
3.3 Collectivism amongst Farmers...................37
3.3.1 Collectivism in Farming.......................37
3.3.2 Cultivating the Fon's Farm....................38
3.3.3 Collectivism during the Construction of Houses.........42
3.3.4 Collectivism during Marriage Ceremonies..............42
3.3.5 Collectivism during Death Celebration.............43
3.4 Conclusion......................................43

Chapter Four: Food Habits and Cooking Methods.................45
4.0 Introduction....................................45
4.1 Method of Preparing *Kɔ̀báyn* 'fufucorn' and *Mbàsɔ̀ ɔ́ Pfíʔɔ̀* 'njamanjama'....................45
4.2 Cassava and it Derivatives......................47
4.3 Preparation of *Nkáŋ* 'corn beer' 49
4.4 Conclusion......................................50

Chapter Five: Crop Cultivation in Kejom Ketinguh..............51
5.0 Introduction....................................51
5.1 Cereals and Legumes.............................55

5.2 Tubers..........58
5.2.1 Cassava..........59
5.2.2 Potatoes..........59
5.3 Market Gardening Crops..........61
5.3.1 Njamanjama..........61
5.3.2 Leeks..........62
5.3.3 Tomatoes..........63
5.3.4 Onion..........63
5.3.5 Other Crops..........64
5.4 Perennial Crops..........65
5.4.1 coffee..........65
5.4.2 Bananas and Plantains..........65
5.4.3 Raffia Palm..........66
5.4.4 Rice..........67
5.5 Conclusion..........68

Chapter Six: Farming Systems..........69
6.0 Introduction..........69
6.1.1 Slash and Burn..........69
6.1.2 Slash and Mulch..........69
6.1.3 Shifting Cultivation..........70
6.1.4 Bush Fallowing..........70
6.1.5 Night Paddock Manuring System..........71
6.1.6 Intensive Rice Farming..........72
6.1.8 Crop Rotation..........73
6.1.9 Fruit Cultivation..........74
6.1.10 Irrigation Farming..........75
6.2 Stages Involved in Farming..........76
6.2.1 Site Selection..........76
6.2.2 Clearing of the Fields..........78
6.2.3 Making Ridges..........78
6.2.4 Sowing or Planting..........78
6.2.5 Weeding..........79
6.2.6 Harvesting..........80

6.2.7 The Agricultural Calendar..................................80
6.3 Conclusion..85

Chapter Seven: Problems Faced By Farmers..................87
7.0 Introduction...87
7.1 Pre-harvest Difficulties...87
7.1.1 Soil Fertility...87
7.1.2 Slope Gradient..87
7.1.3 Pests and Diseases...88
7.1.4 Abandonment of Coffee Farms.............................88
7.1.5 Scare Arable Land...88
7.1.6 Difficult Access to Funds....................................89
7.1.7 Illiteracy and Conservatism.................................89
7.1.8 Farmer-grazier Conflicts.....................................89
7.2 Post-harvest Problems..90
7.2.1 Transportation Difficulties..................................90
7.2.2 Commercialization of the Produce........................91
7.2.3 Poor Storage Facilities.......................................91
7.3 Proposals to Remedy Farming Difficulties in Kejom
    Ketinguh..91
7.3.1 Setting up Cooperatives.....................................92
7.3.2 Adopt the ERI Initiative 93
7.3.3 Create an Agricultural Information Centre for Kejom
    Ketinguh..94
7.4 Conclusion..97

References...98
Web References..100

Appendices..101

List of Figures
Figure 1: Location of Babanki Tungo, North West Region, Cameroon...3
Figure 2 : Structural Genetic Classification of Babanki...........9
Figure 3: Relief Map of Kejom Ketinguh........................20
Figure 4: Farming as a System in Kejom Ketinguh...............52
Figure 5: Soil Occupation in Kejom Ketinguh....................85
Figure 6: A Proposed Agricultural Information Centre in Kejom Ketinguh...96

List of Tables
Table 1: Reign of Kejom Fons and Movement from the Tikari Plain till Date..5
Table 2: Average Temperature and Rainfall Conditions of Kejom Ketinguh from 1995-2005........................18
Table 3: Dominant Agro-pastoral Activities on the Different Relief Units..22
Table 4: Some Commodities Found in Kyephen Market and Sales Pattern...27
Table 5: Main Crops Cultivated in Kejom Ketinguh........53-54
Table 6: Some Major Crop Types in Kejom Ketinguh, Surface Area Covered and Annual Production..................54
Table 7: Annual Output of Crops in Kejom Ketinguh in 2000 and 2012...67
Table 8 : Steps Involved in Rice Cultivation....................73
Table 9 : Agricultural Calendar for some Major Crops in Kejom Ketinguh...82-83

Photos
Photo 1: The Three Stones in Tikebeng from which the Village Name is Derived..21
Photo 2: Rich Volcanic Soils of Mbuandoboh....................23
Photo 3: A Babanki Njamanjama Retail Point in Obili, Yaoundé..29

Photo 4: Menyondo Packaged for Sale...........................49
Photo 5: Mixed Farm at Kumendongmbo....................…..........55
Photo 6. A Mixed Farm in Chua Quarter.. ....….…...56
Photo 7: Maize, Pumpkins and Colocasia Grown on the Same Farm...........…...…...........57
Photo 8: Sweet Potatoes and Potatoes Planted on Separate Sections of the Same Ridges.......................................58
Photo 9: Potato Farm...60
Photo 10: Potatoes Packaged in Bags...........................…......61
Photo 11: Baskets of Tomatoes........................….…...........63
Photo 12: Raffia Bush ....….............…....…...66

Plates
Plate 1: Cassava and Tapioca.................…......…..…........59
Plate 2: Njamanjama..........................….....…….............62
Plate 3: Onion Farm and Harvested Onion....................….........64
Plate 4: Carrots and Cabbages Displayed at the Chuku Market …...…........65
Plate 5: Cattle Pens with and without Cattle...............…........71
Plate 6: Some Wild Fruit in Kejom Ketinguh....................….......74
Plate 7: Irrigation of Farms at Kumendongmbo.................…......75

Preface

Agriculture is the mainstay of the Kejom Ketinguh (Babanki Tungo) economy involving more than 90% of the people. Many people in Cameroon have come to know this village because of its agricultural products, notably the Babanki njamanjama and to a lesser extent the onion, potatoes, and carrots. Even though it is such an important aspect of the people's life, agriculture has remained undeveloped and less productive and has not been documented extensively. It happens that many changes are penetrating the lives of the farmers today with several schools, road connections, electricity, tap water connections, government jobs and several communication tools emerging rapidly. As modernity is closing in swiftly on the people, keeping a record of what they have been doing is indispensable so that after everything has been transformed such a record can still remind the Kejom Ketinguh people of what used to be done in the village in order to sustain lives and move to modernity.

This book contributes to a better understanding of the agricultural activities of the people as those who consume their products in the cities can find in it knowledge of how what they consume is produced. It is also a useful tool for those scholars who are interested in learning about the traditions and culture of this society. This kind of record also makes a significant contribution by proposing new ways for farmers to improve on their activities and move towards better standards of living. There are certainly shortcomings in this book for which the authors accept responsibility and would welcome criticisms and suggestions for improvement.

The collection of information for the writing of this book has been made possible by funds from the Endangered Languages Documentation Program (ELDP). The conception of the book developed from the project "Multimedia

Documentation of Babanki Ritual Speech". As we worked on this project we came to realize that it was necessary to document this important aspect of the life of the people whose language we were documenting.

I would like to express our gratitude to Mr & Mrs Vichas Stephen of GBHS Ndop for taking time to read through the very first draft of this work and making very useful comments and suggestions.

Finally I would like to acknowledge all those people who cultivated the fields whose photographs we have used in this book.

Pius W. Akumbu

CHAPTER ONE
GENERAL INTRODUCTION

1.0 Introduction

When modernity would have completely transformed the life of the Babanki Tungo (henceforth Kejom Ketinguh as the people refer to their village) people, some of the things that might remind them of who they used to be, what they used to do, and how they did it would be written records of their daily activities such as the ones found in this book. The Kejom Ketinguh people live in Tubah subdivision, Mezam Division, Northwest Region of Cameroon and are predominantly farmers who depend on their farm produce to feed themselves and also raise money to meet their financial demands. This book contains a record of this major activity of the people showing especially what they used to do, what is done at present and making suggestions for improvement. The book contains an account of the history of the people as well as their different agricultural activities. It also documents the language used during these activities which are part and parcel of the daily lives of the people. The present chapter contains the geo-historical situation, the linguistic classification of the language, review of literature, motivation, aims and rationale of the study and the layout of the chapters.

1.1 Geo-Historical Situation of Kejom Ketinguh

Kejom Ketinguh is one of the four villages that make up Tubah Sub-Division, Mezam Division, North West Region of Cameroon. It is located between latitudes $5^0 55'$ to $6^0 30'$, north of the Equator and longitudes $10^0 15'$ to $10^0 22'$ East of the Greenwich Meridian (Wuchu, 2011). It is bounded by Bambui to the North, Kejom Keku to the North West, Bamessing to the East, Balikumbat to the South, Bambili and Awing to the West. Less than 15 years ago Kejom Ketinguh had only a few quarters amongst which were Ntehloh, Tualoh, Ntehkezoin, Buh, Techuh, Tingeh, Chuku, Chua, Timenshui and Ketieh (Figure1). As the population has increased enormously, more than 40 other quarters have been created and placed under the leadership of quarter heads. The Fon's palace is located in Ntehloh (quarter of the village). The village occupies an approximated surface area of 125km^2 with a heterogeneous population of about 40.000 people (Akumbu and Fogwe, 2012) comprised of the natives, Mbororo, the Ajung and other Cameroonians who are permanently settled there. This village is located in an area of undulating topography with a major part found in the highlands of Kwighe. The lowland area which is an extension of the Ndop plain covers just Techuh and Ntehkezoin quarters.

There are several ways one can get to Kejom Ketinguh from Bamenda, the regional headquarters of the North West Region. One option is to board a taxi to 'Door Market' through Bambui and Bambili at 600FCFA[1] and then take a motorbike further into the inner parts of the village. Alternatively, one can take a car from Total Nkwen to Tikebeng at 1,200FCFCA or to Timinshui and Chuku in Kwighe at 800FCFA. Access from Ndop costs 500FCFA and from Balikumbat there is a secondary road through Techuh as well as footpaths that lead to the village. The following maps show the location of Kejom Ketinguh clearly.

---

[1] The fares and prices given in this book are those of January, 2015.

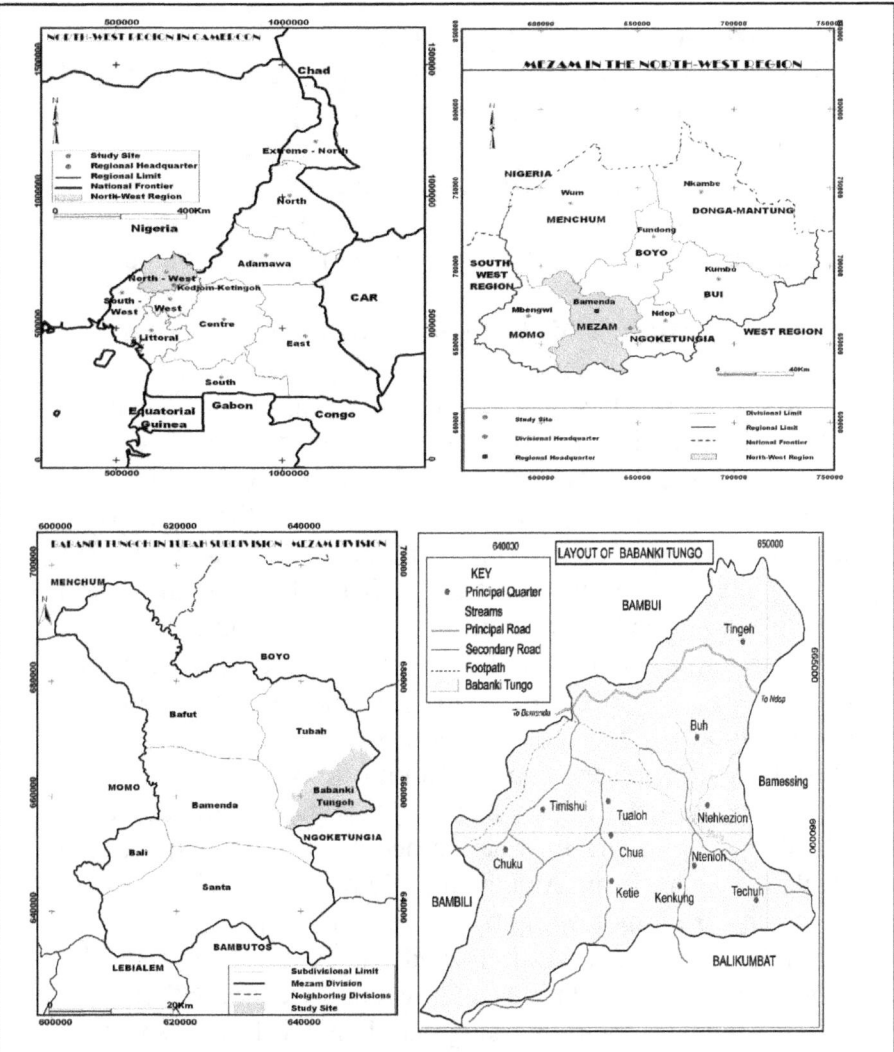

Figure 1: Location of Babanki Tungo, North West Region, Cameroon
Source: CAMGIS DBMS (2013)

1.2 Origin of Kejom Ketinguh Farmers

It should be noted that more than 90% of the inhabitants of Kejom Ketinguh are farmers. With the exception of craftsmen, hunters and those who live out of the village, 9 out of 10 people make their living from cultivating the land. The Kejom people are part of the Tikari ethnic group who moved from around Lake Chad in the 14th century to the present site around the 18th century.

Oral history holds that these people originated from the east of Lake Chad and moved southwards to their present location. The people started migrating around the 14th century and finally settled at their present site around the 18th century. From Chad they moved to the Adamawa, north of Bankim under the reign of Fon Kenhute. They reached the North West Region where they made tours from Belo, Nso, to and from the present site. The group moved together till the reign of Fon Awunti who defied the customs of the land by authorizing the commemoration of an annual dance while the death of a prince was still to be celebrated. This attitude angered some 40 princes who then decided to leave under the leadership of Fon Aseh I to the present site as Kejom Ketinguh. When they arrived the present site they had to gather momentum and fight with their neighbours in order to acquire habitable space and farmland. Apart from Awing and Kejom Keku (from where they split), Kejom Ketinguh has fought with the rest of its neighbours over agricultural land. They clashed with the Bambili people several times and the most recent conflict dates to 1998, and with the Bamessing people in the 1940s as well as with the Balikumbat Fondom. Table (1) illustrates the movement of Kejom people from the Lake Chad area during the 14th century to their present site. The table also shows the different Fons who have ruled the people and their approximate periods of reign.

Name of Fon	Estimated period of rule	Approximate place of rule
Kensante	1400-1425	Around Lake Chad
Kechute	1425-1455	Tikari plain
Kong'aban	1455-1490	Bankim
Akufekong	1490-1530	Near Nso
Fedeng Akang	1530-1560	Kifem
Mbuwain	1560-1580	Around Babessi close to present site Bamoum
Feka'a	1580-1615	Plateau area near Babessi to Nyamisibo
Lye-lye	1615-1645	Oku Land (Jikijem)
Ajoh-Lye	1645-1680	At Nkim Settlement
Azo'o	1680-1705	From Nkim to Kwighe, present day Kejom Ketinguh
Yeea	1705-1740	Timinshui
Anguh	1740-1770	At Tiabongphen
Kebeng	1770-1805	In caves near Babungo, Nkim settlement, Nguesetah
Akumbu	1805-1835	To Belo then back to Kwighe
Yufanyuh	1835-1865	In Kwighe, then to Kom and founded Njinikijem
Awunti	1865-1896	To Kephen, Kefumbum

Fons of Kejom Ketinguh

Aseh I (Aseh Nih) (born in 1796)	1866-1890	Present site
Phunchuh (born in 1811)	1890-1934	Present site
Aseh II (born in 1869)	1934-1961	Present site
Nshiteh (born in 1945)	1961-1981	Present site
Viyuoh (born in 1971)	1981 till date	Present site

Table 1: Reign of Kejom Fons & Movement from the Tikari Plane till Date
Sources: Ntangsi (2000) and Helvetas (2001)

The history of the people is linked to other tribes of Tikar origin. According to oral accounts, the Tikars came from somewhere near the Red sea. They migrated southwards and for some time settled in Tibati, Banyo and Ndobo areas. The Kejom people are amongst the group that settled in Banyo in a place called Kejombeh. They were however forced to move southwards because of invading Fulani tribes.

The Kejom people are the direct descendants of Jom, brother to Moumsi and Nsoh, whose descendants are the Bamoun and the Nso respectively. As far as dates are concerned, Kejom history can actually be traced back to 1400 under the reign of Fon Kensante who ruled till 1425. It is generally held that the Kejom people migrated through Bamoun, Nso to Oku where disagreement with the Oku people over the ownership of the lake, made them move on to Jikejom, one of the significant villages of Oku. Further migration took them through Babessi to Kuwee (present day Chuku in Kejom Ketinguh). Here the Kejom people fought many successful battles, but finally decided to move elsewhere after killing their old men and women whom they considered burdensome and too feeble to fight and buried their durable ornaments.

Their movement took them from Kuwee to Njinikejem in Kom but they soon moved away because of conflicts with the Kom people. While residing in Mbuangang and Muchie in Bafut, their next stop from Kom, a Kejom prince was crowned Fon of Bafut. From Muchie the people moved back to Kuwee, after which they transferred to Kuveshom and later returned to Bafut to a place called Mbuaten. After the death of the ruling Fon, Akumbumade the Kejom people became orphans without a leader. This was due to the fact that the successor, Yufanyu was still a child and so it was suggested that the boy be taken to the Kom Palace to be brought up as a Fon. His people followed him and settled at Njinikejom. When Yufanyu grew up to maturity, he left Kom with his people to Kephem.

It so happened that during the reign of Awunti, successor of Yufanyu, around mid-18th century, when the annual traditional dance was to take place, a prince suddenly died. This raised the question whether the dance should go on first or the prince should be mourned. The final decision to go on with the dance, angered forty princes who split off and moved away with their followers to set up their own Fondom. The forty princes were *Ndifoitein, Tiaku, Ndifonchongong, Mbohnyang, Akuli, Niboh, Sama Kughong, Abuywoh, Samm, Akuh, Kamanbong, Tsuhmbang, Awongie, Ntankgu, Nganyirh, Muwain, Atong, Loh, Akom, Mbiehme, Argubouangie, Mfuhchu, Tinse, Mbain, Vegah, Aswonte, Akungwi, Tengoui, Alufoin, nshom Nsang, Nkwain, Ashigho, Nshom Ngie, Teweyeu, Ngangse, Vefieh, Zhudzang, Muafoin, Lopte, Ninying and Bila.*

When they found themselves at Abongfen, they fought two successive battles against the Mbukwen and Mukung before finally settling near the shrine of their ancestors and called themselves Kejom Ketinguh (Kejom under a stone).

When the Kejom Ketinguh people got to their present site, they crowned Aseh Nih as Fon and planted a fig tree upside down. Its taking root and growing was proof that their ancestors accepted them and they were welcome to settle. The Kejom Ketinguh people made an alliance with the Balikumbat people which permitted them to fight many battles and even succeeded in confiscating the 'kwifoin' of the Babungo people. Their alliance with Balikumbat was finally broken when the Balikumbat people turned around and attacked them for fear that they may grow too powerful.

Aseh Nih became the first Fon of Kejom Ketinguh, while the 40 became the kingmakers. The Fon and the forty constituted the *ŋgyè vú fɔ́yn kɜ̀jɔ̀m* 'house of the original 40' and ruled together. The eldest sons of the 40 together with some village elite were members of the ŋgyè nə̀bɔ̀ʔ 'advisory council' which served as an advisory council to the ŋgyè vú fɔ̀yn kə̀jɔ̀m. Kejom Ketinguh has been ruled by 5 Fons until date (see table 1).

1.3 Linguistic Situation
Víʔə́ kə̀jɔ̀m 'the people of Kejom' speak gáʔə́ kə̀jɔ̀m 'the language of Kejom'. Others call them "Babanki", a designation the people themselves recognize and accept. When speaking with English speakers, they refer to themselves as "Babanki" which is actually the administrative and linguistic name given to them. Ethnologue (2014) lists Babanki with the code ISO 693-3 [bbk] and classifies it as a central Ring language of the wide Grassfields subgroup of Bantoid within Benue-Congo. Following Watters (2003), Babanki can be classified as follows.

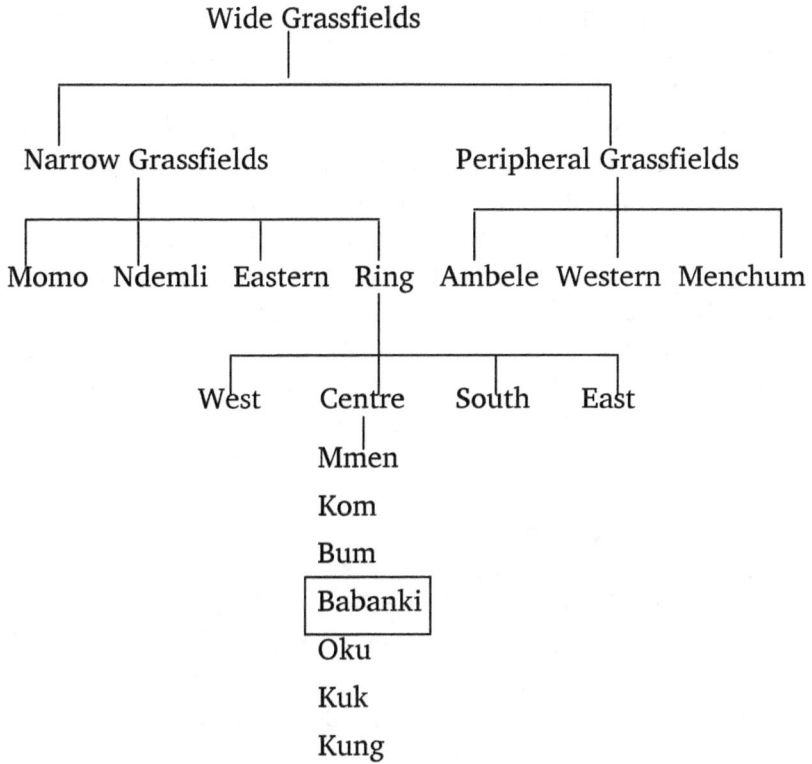

Figure 2 : Structural Genetic Classification of Babanki

Although Cameroon Pidgin has recently spread throughout the village, *Gáʔɔ́ Kɔ́jɔ̀m* is still popular among Kejom Ketinguh people. Those in the village still use the language at homes, in markets, at churches, health centres and in the course of their farming activities. The older people in particular use the language more than the younger ones who tend to use Cameroon Pidgin more. Less than 20 years ago the people in Tikebeng used Pidgin more than those in Kwighe because the former parts had contact with foreigners before the latter part. When people from Kwighe visited Tikebeng they were easily recognized and considered to be 'primitive' based on the fact that they couldn't speak Cameroon Pidgin. This is no longer the case today because both parts of the village are now open to civilization and modernity and the distinction is fast disappearing. One factor that has accelerated the loss of the language has been the spread of formal education with several primary and secondary schools that the children attend. Although *Gáʔə́ Kə̀jɔ̀m* is seriously threatened there is still hope that the language will still be transmitted to the next generation especially because there are efforts to document and preserve the language (Akumbu, 2014)[2] and the Bible is currently being translated into the language. This is particularly so because Bible translation is also accompanied by literacy classes to train the people to read and write *Gáʔə́ Kə̀jɔ̀m*.

1.4 Literature Review

In this part we present some of the previous studies that have been done on the Kejom Ketinguh community ranging from studies on language, to those on agricultural practices and culture to show that this work is actually an innovation since no other research has focused on this aspect of the people's life.

1.4.1 Language

By the late 1970s researchers began to take interest in the study of the Kejom language (Babanki) and since then many linguistic analyses of the language have been done.

Hyman (1979) proposes an abstract analysis to account for a number of intricate tonal alternations found in Babanki nouns. This analysis makes use of floating tones in underlying forms differing markedly from their surface realizations. He

---

[2] This project to document the language of ritual speech in Kejom Ketinguh from January to December, 2014 is sponsored by the Endangered Languages Documentation Programme (ELDP), SOAS London.

postulates ten ordered tone rules that essentially recapitulate the tonal history of the language.

Hyman (1980) undertakes a study of the noun class system of Babanki. He compares Babanki and other Ring languages and ends up reconstructing the proto-Ring noun class system based on the comparative data.

Menang (1981), proposed an analysis of the language spoken by "Nakang", (a juju in Babanki). He illustrates the differences between this restricted dialect and the ordinary day-to-day language of the people and exposes some of the connotative meanings that arise from this special usage.

Menang (1983) undertakes an elementary study of the word class in Babanki paying much attention to the nouns alongside their concord systems.

Tamanji (1987) provides a phonological description of the language, taking into consideration the possible combination of sounds into syllables, morphemes and words. Using the structuralist approach to phonological analysis, he focuses mainly on the sound system, presenting the segmental and supra-segmental phonemes of the language. This study also proposes an alphabet and orthographic principles for the writing of Babanki.

Akumbu (1999) identifies and describes phonological processes that occur within the nouns of Babanki. Using the generative approach, he captures changes that occur within the nouns in isolation, as well as at phrasal level.

Phubon (1999) contains a study of the phonological system in Babanki, with particular emphasis laid on the phonological rules that relate postulated underlying forms to the phonetic forms. However, because of the purpose of the work she concentrates only on the behaviour of nouns leaving out other categories.

Phubon (2002) attempts an identification and explanation of the phonological and tonological processes that occur within the verb in Babanki. One of the major findings of the work is that the verb in this language exhibits two tonal levels, high and low. The other tonal melodies, mid, rising and falling are derived through tonological processes.

Mutaka & Phubon (2006) present a situation of vowel raising in the language in which the back vowels, *a, o* alternate with *o, u*, respectively in genitive and possessive constructions as well as in certain verbal constructions just in the case they are part of the sequence *Vŋ* (where V stands for vowel). In the analysis they propose that vowel raising is the result of the association of the floating features [+hi, +ATR, -bk] which constitute the underlying features of the vowel *i* that never surfaces after the *ŋ* sound. In the analysis, they also exploit the feature make-up of the vowels as underlyingly underspecified.

Phubon (2007) using both the autosegmental framework and the lexical phonology model, identifies and explains some phonological and tonological processes that occur in this language. The work provides evidence that prior to affixation of stratum one formatives, the underived lexical item (root) is scanned by the phonology. She proves that the stem (i.e. the root and final vowel (FV)) and the subject marker are derived at stratum one. The pre-stem material, that is, the subject marker and the tense markers, as well as the noun class prefix undergo stratum two rules. These two strata are claimed to be autonomous blocks with their own properties.

In the domain of lexicography, Akumbu (2008) has compiled the Kejom (Babanki) –English lexicon. He collects over 2000 entries that serve as an introduction to Babanki words and phrases. This provisional lexicon has been compiled for the speakers of Babanki, though it is also of interest to non-speakers who desire to study or learn the language. This lexicon is seen as a step forward in the preservation of the cultural identity of the Babanki people, which is facing extinction as we evolve. This lexicon, as envisaged, will be used as a reference material in standardizing the spelling of Babanki words and terminology.

Akumbu (2009) identifies and describes the two grammatical categories in Babanki that are used for temporal specification (tense and aspect), and also demonstrates in the paper that there is a co-occurrence constraint that operates between tense and the time adverbials they occur with.

Akumbu (2011), unlike Hyman (1979), proposes a synchronic account of tone in the Babanki associative construction within the framework of Register Tier Theory, making use of only a few tone rules. He concludes that the behaviour of tones in the associative construction is conditioned by the presence of a nasal in the onset position of the juxtaposed noun roots.

Without using any specific formal model Akumbu and Fogwe (2012) provide a description of the grammar of Babanki in a way that it will be useful to the learners and teachers of the language, as well as to others interested in this and other Grassfields Bantu languages.

1.4.2 Agriculture

In contrast, agriculture, being the backbone of the economy of the village has received only little attention from writers. The few works in which some aspects of agricultural practices within Kejom Ketinguh have been discussed are the following.

CIPCRE (2014), in an article entitled *"Auto-prise en charge des populations"* presents the success of efforts of the local Kejom Ketinguh people in enhancing agricultural productivity. The article notes that due to pressure on land and reduction in soil fertility, the people of Kejom Ketinguh in an effort to incorporate livestock to farming have developed a farming system called "night paddocking manuring farming" which has considerably improved productivity especially in areas of market gardening. The system is today practised in many areas of the North West region.

Velem (2013), on the other hand bases his research on the influence of relief on land use in Kejom Ketinguh. His main concern is on how relief influences agricultural practices in Kejom Ketinguh, considering that the village has two distinct relief features -a lowland and a highland. He concludes that there is a significant relationship between relief and farming systems as well as the type of crops grown in the village. This is so because the relief, in turn, influences the climate and soils of the different relief units.

Wombong (2003) on his part takes interest on man's activities in Babanki Tungo and examines how man uses the soils in Babanki Tungo for his livelihood. The author describes a pattern of agricultural practice in the village where market gardening activities dominate in the upper sections of the village while those in the lower part of the village, on their part, concentrate on cultivating cassava as the main cash crop. Since many of the villagers are involved in cultivating one market gardening crop or the other the author notes that the agricultural landscape of the village is rich in diversity as far as crop cultivation is concerned. The people also use their land for livestock activities such that cattle, pigs, goats, chickens, rabbits, etc are reared across the entire village.

1.4.3 Culture

As far as the culture of the Kejom people is concerned, the only work we are aware of is that done by Ntangsi (2000) who describes some socio-cultural aspects of Kejom Ketinguh. He provides a brief account of the history of the people before discussing the nature of traditional marriage in Kejom which starts with courtship, self-introduction and the creation of alliances. He notes that many aspects of the traditional marriage have been affected negatively by modernism. The author equally discusses the significance of roasted chicken and taboos related to it and also sheds light on traditional reproductive health practices. The cultural role and manifestation of ə̀fó ə́ ntə̀? 'quarter things' is equally discussed. ə̀fó ə́ ntə̀? is an expectation among some youth that a young girl is supposed to have sex with at least a boy from the quarter where she grew up before going to marriage, thereby giving a share of herself to that quarter.

The literature review shows that the present study which incorporates a wide range of the agricultural life of the people is also unique in discussing aspects of the use of language in the agricultural practices, an issue that has not been addressed in any previous research.

1.5 Motivation

The authors of this book were born and raised in Kejom Ketinguh and almost everyone around them was involved in farming. They themselves owned a few ridges or entire fields at their young ages. They saw their parents repeat the farming cycle year after year and they grew up depending on the food from the family fields for feeding and raising of money for their education. As they look back at those years of tilling, harvesting, transporting and as they see their other family members who still continue with the same activities and especially their parents who have been doing it for close to a century they agree that it is necessary to document these activities that are part of the livelihood of themselves and their fellow people.

1.6 Aims and Rationale

This book is meant to document the agricultural practices of the Kejom Ketinguh people while paying attention to their use of the Kejom language in the process. As modernity is closing in rapidly on the people, keeping a record of what they have been doing is indispensable so that after everything has been modified or modernized such a record can still remind the Kejom Ketinguh people of what used to be done in the village in order to sustain lives and move to modernity. It is also hoped that such a record can make a significant contribution by proposing new ways for farmers to improve on their activities and move towards better standards of living. This book will certainly contribute to a better understanding of the agricultural activities of the people and those who consume their products in the cities will have a better knowledge of how what they consume is produced and then be able to value the items more.

1.7   Layout of the Work

This work is presented in seven chapters. Chapter one contains the geo-historical and linguistic situation of Kejom Ketinguh, the review of work done on the language, agriculture and culture, the motivation for the study as well as the aims and rationale of the work. Chapter two on its part exposes the factors that favour the practice of agriculture and its productivity while the general life of the farmers of the village is discussed in the third chapter. The fourth chapter gives insights of food habits and methods of preparing some commonly consumed food items in Kejom Ketinguh. The different crops cultivated are presented in the fifth chapter while chapter six focuses on farming systems and the different stages involved in farming in Kejom Ketinguh. Chapter seven rounds off with the problems that affect agriculture in this village as well as the possible solutions that can be adopted in order to improve on agricultural productivity in the village.

CHAPTER TWO
AGRICULTURAL PRODUCTIVITY

2.0 Introduction

Agricultural activities in this Kejom Ketinguh are determined and controlled by a number of factors. These factors influence productivity as well as the form of agriculture practised. There are two sets of conditions that influence agriculture in this village, namely, physical or natural, and human and economic factors.

2.1 Physical or Natural Factors

The physical or natural factors that foster agricultural productivity here include favourable climatic conditions, the topography, soils and vegetation. These factors promote agricultural activities in Kejom Ketinguh as demonstrated below.

2.1.1 Favourable Climatic Conditions

Kejom Ketinguh has a varied climate within its geographic area because of its topography of hills and plains. The highest temperatures are registered in the lower part of Kejom Ketinguh, which lies in the Ndop plain. Kwighe and all the upper parts of Kejom Ketinguh, generally have lower temperatures. These climatic variations fit into two distinct seasons- the rainy season that stretches from mid-March to the later part of October and is characterized by heavy rains ushered in by the south west monsoon winds. Although places are generally wet during this period, temperatures are relatively high (table 2). The dry season runs from November to mid-March and is marked by the harmattan.

Climatic elements							Months						
		J	F	M	A	M	J	J	A	S	O	N	D
Temp.(°C)	Max.	25.4	26.5	25.3	24.5	22.6	22.9	21.8	21.1	18.6	19.3	20.2	22.6
	Min.	11.2	12.0	14.6	15.7	14.6	14.4	14.6	14.5	12.5	12.5	12	11.0
	Mean	18.3	19.3	19.9	20.1	18.6	18.9	18.2	17.8	17.8	15.5	16.1	16.8
Rainfall (mm)	Monthly Averages	0	0	112.2	163.4	172.9	234.2	318.6	358.4	258.9	215.1	0	0
Evaporation (mm)	Monthly Averages	131.7	162.4	141	130.5	136.4	119	96	93	96	114.7	103	114.7

Table 2: Average Temperature and Rainfall Conditions of Kejom Ketinguh from 1995-2005
Source: Bamenda Airport Meteorological Data 1995-2005

The table shows that the dry season is short and lasts for four months from mid-October to mid-March. This dry season corresponds to the periods of harvest for some crops such as beans, potatoes, cocoyams, sweat potatoes and market gardening crops. The rainy season is long, running from mid-march to mid-October with the heaviest rainfall recorded in August. The climate in this area usually experiences temperature and rainfall variations and this gives rise to a good drainage system that encourages the cultivation of market gardening crops.

The upper section of Kejom Ketinguh has a mean maximum temperature of 20-22°C while its minimum ranges from 13°C to 14°C. December records the lowest minimum temperatures while February records the highest maximum temperatures. Rainfall varies from 1,780mm to 2,290mm per year. Most rain falls between July and September. January and February have the lowest relative humidity (45-52%) and the highest evaporation rates. The lowest evaporation rates are in August. The plain area is hot and sunny with mean annual maximum temperatures between 27-33°C and a rainfall of 1,270-1,778mm.

2.1.2   Topography or Relief

The relief of Kejom Ketinguh shows two distinctive features, a plateau and a plain. The plateau constitutes the area called Kwighe. It is found at a high attitude between 1,600m and 2,400m. It is characterized by hills, interlocking spurs, knolls, escarpments and slopes and demarcated by woody valleys. The relief is so rough in some areas particularly escarpments presenting a natural barrier to human occupation. The hills here provide a real watershed for the area. The relief is shown in figure 3.

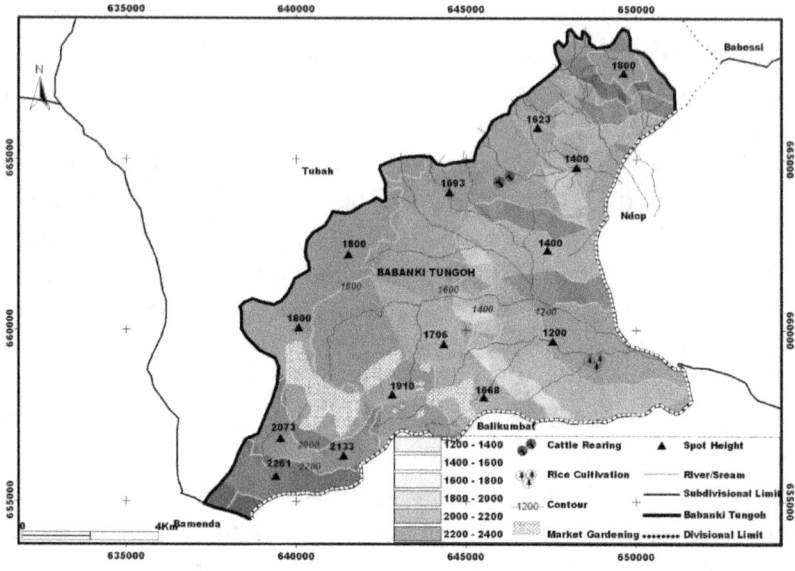

Figure 3: Relief Map of Kejom Ketinguh
Source: CAMGIS DBMS (2013)

The lower part of the village constitutes the plain and is called Tikebeng. The plain is located at an average elevation of 1180m and covers Techuh, Tekuh, Buh and part of Ntehkezoin quarters. It should be noted that this lower part of the village area equally has s series of hills including the three hills or stones from where the village got its name. The three stones are ŋgùʔɜ̀àsɨ̀ʔ 'Aseh's stone', ŋgùʔɜ̀mbɔ́ʔnyáŋ 'Mbohnyang's stone' and ŋgùʔɜ̀bjí 'Bji's stone'. This area is drained by the Noun River and is liable to seasonal flooding. The following photograph shows part of the topography of Tikebeng including the three hills.

⟶ ŋgùʔəmbɔ́ʔnyáŋ ⟶ ŋgùʔɔ̀àsɨ̀ʔ ⟶ ŋgùʔɔ̀bjí
Photo 1: The Three Stones in Tikebeng from which the Village Name is Derived

Kejom Ketinguh has 14 water falls (Helvetas monographic study of Tubah, 2001) and 2 main streams that are fed by feeder brooks from the upland plateau. The streams are Foynkom and Mughom. The streams are fast flowing due to the slope gradient towards the Ndop plain. At their merging point the Upper Noun Valley Development Authority (UNVDA) has constructed a dam to serve the rice fields at Techuh. During the rainy season, sediments are eroded from the upper plateau down to the plain where alluvial deposits are formed.

The physical environment plays an important role in determining agricultural activities. In effect, agricultural activities vary from the talweg to the summit (table 3).

Dominant activities	Relief unit
Considered communal property used for agro-pastoral activities and gathering.	summits and plateau
Grazing, hunting, and grass cutting for thatching.	steep slopes with rock out crop
Arable farming, animal husbandry, bee keeping quarrying.	gentle slopes
Intensive arable farming irrigated gardening, poultry piggery.	low lands and stream valleys

Table 3: Dominant Agro-pastoral Activities on the Different Relief Units
Source: Adapted from Wuchu (2011) and 2014 field work

It can be observed from the table that the topography of the area contributes to the diversification of agricultural activities.

2.1.3 Suitable Soil Conditions

Kejom Ketinguh has soils which are considerably fertile. This is the base of agricultural activities for the people. The fertility of the soils is due to the abundance of humus, which is a dark volcanic soil found up the hills of Kejom Ketinguh. The soils here are dark clay especially in areas such as Mbuandoboh and Kumedongmbo. The soils are moderately deep and well drained and have high organic matter contents.

Photo 2: Rich Volcanic Soils of Mbuandoboh

The photograph depicts a sample of soil within the farming basin of Mbuandoboh characterized by dark deep volcanic soils. These soils are very fertile and thanks to improved irrigation techniques farming is done in this area all year round.

The lower part of Kejom Ketinguh has mainly hydromorphic soils, formed from the annual deposits of sediments from the upper plateau. The top soil here is silt loam with much organic matter while the sub soil is silky clay loam. The moisture content is abundant even during the dry season, about 19.35%. Due to the flatness of the topography, the availability of water and high contents of organic matter, the hydromorphic soils are of good quality. There is a bit of sandy soil washed down from the hills and deposited on the riverbeds or banks of streams. This type of soil is used for the construction of houses. In order to enhance soil fertility the farmers use compose manure, wood ash, droppings from cattle, goats, guinea pigs and chickens. In some instances the *mfwĭ* 'ankara' is constructed to obtain fertile soils even if the effect is usually short lived. Some go for fallow with some shrubs planted on the portions under fallow. Their fallen leaves permit the soil to regain fertility.

2.1.4 Suitable Vegetation

Kejom Ketinguh is located in the savanna belt and the rich soil presents a good environment for lush grass to grow. A good portion of the village had been covered with trees a long time ago especially the upper section of the village but apart from a few forest patches there are virtually no natural forests left. Tall grass covers most of the hills dotted with stunted shrubs providing good grazing land. In the dry season, the grass quickly dries up; however the rice fields and surrounding lowland areas are used for transhumance. This vegetation eases opening up of farms within the village.

2.2 Human and Economic Factors

The human environment of Kejom Ketinguh complements the suitable natural conditions to boost agricultural activities in this village. Amongst these conditions, are the presence of many research centres and NGOs. The available markets, some farm to market roads and a good labour-force can also be considered as favourable conditions for agriculture.

2.2.1 The Role of Research Centres and NGOs

The government extension workers and training centre of IRAD-Bambui and the Agriculture School of Bambili as well as the Presbyterian Rural Training Centre, Nfonta are training institutions for farmers in Tubah sub-division which have been at the service of the Kejom people. Apart from these research and training institutions, there are also NGOs both local and international that work towards the improvement of the living conditions of the rural population of Kejom Ketinguh through agriculture. The institutions include:

2.2.1.1 Livelihood NGO

This is an NGO sponsored by Helvetas Cameroon. In 1997, Livelihood NGO carried out training and sensitization on conservation farming systems in Kejom Ketinguh. In 1998, it carried out general sensitization on the importance of natural resource management and watershed management in Kejom Ketinguh and Kejom Keku. Demonstration farms for mushroom and vegetables as well as home gardens were established and many Kejom Ketinguh people received training. Livelihood was also involved in soil and water conservation farming systems, and did water catchment protection work in Tingeh and Chuku. By the year 2000, the activities of the local NGO spread over Tubah sub-division with training on seed selection, prevention of post-harvest loss, conservation farming system, mushroom cultivation, vegetable farming and tree planting techniques.

2.2.1.2 Cercle International Pour la Production et de la Création (CIPCRE)

This is an NGO with its headquarters in Bafoussam and a branch office in Bamenda. It has trained farmers in mixed farming and sustainable crop and animal production. In Kejom Ketinguh, they have instituted an efficient night paddock manuring system. In the 1990s this NGO encouraged farmers to get into farming groups and under their supervision over 52 farming groups specialized in the production of different crops were set up.

2.2.1.3 Helvetas Cameroon

This is the most popular international NGO operating in Kejom Ketinugh. It intervenes directly in some projects and also through local NGOs like livelihood, PEMSAHR, HURCLED centre which have executed pasture improvement projects, agricultural projects, environmental projects, and promotion of education and human rights in the village.

2.2.1.4 Heifer Project International (H.P.I)

Heifer Project International has done much in Kejom Ketinguh imparting farming techniques to women groups and introducing improved dairy cows and small livestock such as goats and pigs. They have equally provided seeds for pasture improvement. Their system of assistance known as *pass on gift* (POG) helps in faster acquisition of animals by other villagers.

2.2.1.5 Other NGOs

Other NGOs also actively involved in promoting the agricultural sector in Kejom Ketinguh are INADES, PAFSAT and GIZ.

INADES formation focuses on the training of farmers and for many years has been actively involved in the village, training several farmers.

PAFSAT on its part encouraged farmers to use cattle and cart for tilling the soil and to use high yielding seed varieties.

GIZ in collaboration with the Tinguh Cooperative Credit Union Limited (TICCUL) has been actively involved in assisting farmers. In 2010 they organized training seminars on doing business as a farmer. They gave lectures on managing farms as an enterprise, adding value through quality production, basics on healthy nutrition and food security.

2.2.2 Available Markets

Kejom Ketinguh has a population of over 40.000 inhabitants. This is a great market for the local produce. However the different villages that surround the village such as Balikumbat, Bamessing, Bambili and Bambui constitute another segment of the market. The village is equally close to the regional headquarter, Bamenda, being less than 20km away and benefits largely from the proximity. There is however no market that operates on a daily basis in this village. There are three major markets on *əmbíwí* (Tikebeng), Kyephen (door market near Tingeh) and on Fridays at Chuku (Yoruba market in Kwighe). Buyers converge from several parts of the Region and even beyond to buy directly from farmers during these three market days. These main markets have virtually the same agricultural and animal products. Table (4) shows commodities that are often brought to the Kyephen market and the sales pattern.

No	Commodity produced	Quantity	Average unit price	Total value of goods	Quantity Sold
1	bananas	20 bunches	300	6,000	all
2	plantains	62 bunches	800	49,600	all
3	cocoyams	6 buckets	2,000	12,000	all
4	potatoes	10 buckets	2,200	22,000	all
5	sweet potatoes	12 buckets	800	9,600	all
6	maize	12 buckets	1,800	21,600	all
7	beans	14 buckets	3,500	49,000	8 buckets
8	rice	10 bags	14,000	140,000	3 bags
9	Tapioca (garri)	12 bags	8,000	96,000	8 bags
10	tomatoes	32 buckets	2,000	64000	all
11	carrots	8 buckets	2,000	16,000	5 buckets
12	local breed chicken	14	2,500	35,000	9
13	soya beans	12 bags	8,000	96,000	5 bags

Table 4: Some Commodities Found in Kyephen Market and Sales Pattern
Source: Market survey and market master's records, October 2013

From the table we observe that most of what is brought into the market is sold completely. Just a few commodities go back home. This is an encouragement for them to produce more.

There are shift markets in the village, which appear spontaneously and maybe short lived. Some have lasted for quite some time and may eventually become permanent. Such markets include *Bobi Na One* in Timinshui, and the Ketieh Market. Others operate in front of churches on Sundays or on some spots where buyers and sellers happen to be or simply develop along the road to sell to travelers. Thus spots along the road to Ndop from Bamenda (e.g. *Door Market*) have retailers throughout the day selling crops and vegetables.

Apart from the internal and road side markets, Kejom Ketinguh is blessed to be on part of the Bamenda Ring road. The village serves the main markets of Bamenda town, Bambui and Ndop with a good number of crops and animal products. It is equally common to find market gardening products from Kejom Ketinguh in major cities in Cameroon. This is the case of the famous '*Babanki njamanjama*[3]' in Douala and Yaoundé. This vegetable is even sold in international markets such as in Equatorial Guinea. The following photograph shows women trading in this delicacy in the heart of Yaoundé.

---

[3] Njamanjama is the popular local name of the dark green leafy vegetable which some people in Cameroon call huckleberry.

Photo 3: A Babanki Njamanjama Retail Point in Obili, Yaoundé

This is one of the retail points of the Babanki njamanjama at Carrefour Obili in Yaoundé. The vegetable is taken to Yaoundé, usually during night journeys, maybe in order to preserve the quality of the njamanjama and also to make the vegetable available to customers very early in the morning. Retailers converge at travel agencies such as Amour Mezam, Guarantee, and Vatican to collect the njamanjama and take to the different retail points. This operation is done on a daily basis and this njamanjama can be found in restaurants, and many households around the niegbourhoods of BiyemAssi, Obili, Ekounou, Essos and even Soa in the outskirts of Yaoundé.

2.2.3   Road Infrastructure
Kejom has a portion of tarred road, starting from its boundary with Bambili to the boundaries with Ndop Sub-Division at Bamessing.

Apart from the tarred road, earth roads have either been built by the community or with community participation. The community uses basic instruments such as hoes and spades to dig roads. Footpaths are equally numerous, making all the quarters of the village accessible either on foot or in some cases by motorbikes and cars.

The main vehicles that ply the roads are taxis from Bamenda town. Motor bikes are very popular and ply especially the earth roads and footpaths. Several big trucks pass through taking finished products to or raw materials from Ngoketunjia, Bui and Donga Mantung divisions.

2.3 Conclusion

In this chapter it has been demonstrated that agricultural activities thrive in Kejom Ketinguh because of natural, human and economic factors. The favourable climatic conditions, the topography or relief, as well as suitable soil conditions and vegetation on the one hand and the influence of research centres and NGOs, the availability of markets, proximity to the main tarred road (Ring Road) and the existence of manpower all work in favour of agriculture.

CHAPTER THREE
GENERAL LIFE OF FARMERS

3.0 Introduction

The day to day life of a typical Kejom Ketinguh person is centred around farming and even those who engage in carving and hunting also own farms and cultivate several kinds of crops. Most of the food eaten in the village is produced locally and occasionally the people sell some of their produce in order to buy the rest of the things they need to complement their living. Children are brought up within this context and farming becomes part of their normal habits and those who are considered to be rich normally have large farms. Sometimes in order for the family heads to increase their labour force they resort to getting more than one wife. For example one of the most influential farmers in Chuku, has eleven wives with several children and, therefore, can afford to own many large farms. Many instances of men marrying several wives in order to increase their labour force are common in the village and widespread especially around the Chuku quarter. The bond of kinship is strongly maintained and the whole village is directly or indirectly related to each other, either through patrilineal or matrimonial alliances. In this chapter we present ways and means of protection used by the people to secure their crops from evil spirits, animals and birds as well as from thieves and also discuss how collectivism is manifested amongst them.

3.1 Rituals Leading to the Planting Season

There are three remarkable stages involved in the rituals leading to the planting season in Kejom Ketinguh. These rituals usually take place in the later part of *sàŋə̀ kə̀ ntólìm* 'February' each year. The different events are: *bvàʔə̀ tə̀fám* 'shrine sacrifice', *mɔ̀ʔə̀ vənyìŋgɔ̀ŋ* 'sacrificing to the gods' and *kə̀bénkə́ vənyìŋgɔ̀ŋ* 'sacrifice celebration dance festival'. After the dance festival the farmers go into their farms for planting with a lot of anxiety and hope for high yields.

3.1.1 Bvàʔə̀ Tə̀fám 'shrine sacrifice'

This is a ritual exercise that takes place in shrines dotted at the boundaries and entrances into the village. The *tə̀fám* 'shrines' are located at Chuku, Tingeh (border with Bambili), Mbuandoboh (border with Balikumbat and Awing), Tiku (border with Bamessing and Balikumbat). Some of the *tə̀fám* are located within the village at Fendieng, and Ntehloh just at the entrance to the palace. This exercise is done by a sacred cult called *ŋgàŋ* in order to protect and prevent all forms of evil from coming into the village. The ritual destroys the powers of anything evil and counterproductive that any person tries to bring into the village. After this they can then go into sacrificing and appeasing the gods of the lands.

3.1.2 Mɔ̀ʔə̀ Və̀nyìŋgɔ̀ŋ 'sacrificing to the gods'

This ritual is carried out by another sacred group called *və̀pfèm*. Their major activity is to feed the gods and plead for protection, provision and productivity. The major requirements for this particular ritual are:
- *kə̀làŋ* 'achu (pounded cocoyams)'
- *ŋkúf* 'raffia palm'
- *byì* 'red camwood'
- *ə̀fú ə́ mbŭmbù* 'special leaf'
- *mbvúsə́* 'chickens'
- *byísə́* 'goats'
- *ŋgə̀ʔsə́* 'egusi'

Preparations usually start on wyéŋgáŋ '2nd weekday', with queens preparing the achu, egusi and others while the Fon slaughters the chickens himself. On the following day àjùŋ '3rd weekday', the members of *və̀pfə̀m* go into activity. They go out to every corner of the village where these gods are located to feed them. To keep themselves pure and ritually clean and prepared for the exercise *vàpfèm* members are not allowed to have contact with any woman.

The gods of Kejom Ketinguh are usually symbolized by a small stone lying on a larger one either on caves, lake sides, forests, water bodies, around big stones and backyards of some compounds. Some of the gods include:

i. *nyìngɔ̀ŋ ɔ̀ ŋgyɨ́ŋgì* located at the former palace site at Mbuaten quarter. This is a god of fertility amongst the people of Kejom Ketinguh.
ii. *nyìngɔ̀ŋ ɔ̀ mó* at the lake side at Chuku who is responsible for rainfall.
iii. *nyìngɔ̀ŋ ɔ̀ kɔ̀chʉ́ kɔ́ fífɔ́kɔ́* located at *ŋgùʔɔ̀ àsɨ̀ʔ*, one of the stones from which the village derived its name. It is found close to the palace.
iv. *nyìngɔ̀ŋ ɔ̀ ntúʔ* is located inside the palace itself. It is actually the skull of one of the founders of the village and it's role is to protect the village.
v. *nyìngɔ̀ŋ ɔ̀ fyɔ bàŋɔ́ ghɔ́* located at the red cave at Buh.

It can be observed that the gods of Kejom Ketinguh are fairly distributed all over the village and this explains why the *vàpfɔ̀m* are usually assigned to go to the different quarters to identify the gods and appease them. They make sure they do not forget any god because if they do, the consequences could be disastrous.

The incantation that goes with the feeding process is as follows:

vɔ̀nyìngɔ̀ŋ vyɔ́sɔ́ ghɔ̀ŋ gháʔ mɔ̀nlyúʔ mɔ̀ ntúʔ mɔ̀n ɔ̀ tsɨ̀ŋɔ̀ ɔ̀lɔ́ʔ ɔ́ kɔ́jɔ̀m, ɔ̀ kù ɔ́wʉ́ ghɔ́ gyámtɔ́ ɔ́fó kwí á ŋkàyn. Kwùʔsɔ́ vʉ́nɔ́ à jès ɔ̀ bwàʔsɔ́ víʔɔ́ kɔ́jɔ̀m á ɔ́lɔ́ʔ bènɔ́ á ɔ̀tím nɔ̀ ɔ̀nwʉ́ vɔ̀wé nɔ́ʔɔ̀ vɔ̀tsèm.

"gods of our land receive this wine from the Fon and protect our land from all evil, give us abundant rain for our crops to grow, so that we can have a good harvest. Give us more children and prosper all the villagers in and out of the village and bless them in what they do'.

They say this while pouring the wine on the stones that represent the gods, putting a bit of camwood, pieces of chicken, achu and egusi on each *mbŭmbù* leaf and placing them on the larger stone. The smaller stone is placed on the leave with the food items and more palmwine is poured on everything.

As they go along doing this they rub camwood on the forehead of any villager they meet provided the villager wishes to identify with the blessings of the gods.

At the end of the day, all the *vɔ̀pfɔ̀m* converge at the palace to commence the *kɔ̀bénkɔ́ vɔ̀nyìŋgɔ̀ŋ* 'sacrifice celebration dance festival'. This dance is simply the celebration of the appeasement process and appreciation to the gods for answering their prayers.

At the end of the dance, which usually goes on for three days, the farmers proceed to plant their crops. They do this with confidence that they are protected from all forms of evil and, in addition, they expect a good harvest and an increase in the fertility of the population.

The use of language in the incantations reflects the fact that the people have put their trust in the gods of their land and are convinced that their safety, survival and success depend only on the goodwill of those gods.

3.2 Protection of Farms by the Population
Kejom people believe that witchcraft, evil and good spirits exist. Therefore, in spite of the general action by the Fon in the

appeasement of the gods, farmers might still get into trouble. That is why they can further seek and implement other protective measures.

3.2.1 Protection from Witchcraft and Evil Spirits

Evil spirits are generally believed to move in strong winds. They come either to destroy crops of all sorts or houses. The people have their way of protecting their farms against such spirits. They mix up some concoctions in the form of either *kə̀fú kə́ njú* 'medicine of honesty', or *kə̀fú kə́ fénə́kə́* 'black medicine' also called *kə̀fú kə́ ákúə̀* 'Aku's medicine' named after the former custodian, late Pa Aku. The mixture is then rubbed on elephant grass storms, and each is interwoven on the four corners of the plot as well as in the centre. *Njìbàŋ*, a plant species is planted on the ridges particularly in the case where njamanjama is the main vegetable in the farm. This goes with incantations such as follows:

və̀nyìŋgɔ̀ŋ vyə́sə́, və̀nyìgɔ̀ŋ və́ və̀tì?ə́ vyə́sə́, ghə̀ŋ tsíŋə́ ə̀sím yénə́ fà və̀zhí nə̀ ə̀zhwí byívə́ ə̀ nè lá tà ə̀zhwí djúŋə́və́ ə́ndí? à shə̀ ndì?í ə̀fó vwɔ́mə́ né á ŋkàyn.

'gods of our land, of our forefathers, protect this plot from evil spirits so that crops should not be destroyed and that only good spirits should stay around so that I should have a good harvest'.

It must be mentioned that this practice is no longer popular as the wind of Christianity has blown through the entire village, causing people to rather put their trust and dependence on God rather than on the gods and sacrifices. Modernity and formal education have also contributed to diminishing the impact of traditional belief and trust in the gods.

3.2.2 Protection from Wild Animals and Birds

Wild animals such as rat moles, squirrels, and monkeys as well as birds like partridges either dig up planted seeds or eat crops at every stage of their growth. In this case the farmers have to devise some measures, including the setting of traps (*màntómà, fùmə́lā?*, etc) to catch animals or they use images to scare away animals. The *kə̀mbáŋsə̀* "frightening image", some of them representing human beings are placed around the farm and some really scare away most of the animals. Other people opt for their children to go and guide the farms at regular intervals by simply making noise or lighting up a fire to send out smoke from the farm houses giving the impression that there is someone around. This also scares away some wild animals. In addition, fences are built around the farm to prevent cattle, goats and other animals from going in and eating up the crops.

3.2.3 Protection from Thieves

The farmers watch out and make sure that they keep the boundaries of their farms clear of grass and trees so that they can easily see from afar. They can protect the farms with *chísə́* 'afflictions' such as *ə̀chə̀m, fə̀ŋkílím, ə̀lyə́ŋ ə́ nsú?, chì*, etc. All of these are diseases that the custodians can afflict thieves or enemies with and can also easily provide remedies for when the victim owns up and apologizes. If any of these afflictions is placed in a farm and someone harvests anything from that farm they will be affected by the disease. When thieves see any of these in a farm they avoid stealing from such farms.

Late Pa Nkwenti of Chua was noted for inflicting *ndàŋ* 'filaria' and *ə̀bə̀m ə́ nzím* 'dry stomach' on anyone who stole his sugarcane or guava. He would place the concoction in the farm and anyone who harvests anything from there will be afflicted immediately. Several accounts are given of people who stole from his farms and felt the obligation to run to him and confess so that he could heal them. When they got to him he will expose them to everyone as the thief and then beat them up severely before giving them the necessary treatment. As soon as he gave them the treatment they got instant relief.

3.3 Collectivism amongst Farmers

It is impossible to live in isolation without the help and cooperation of the other villagers. In Kejom Ketinguh there is cohabitation of the rich and the poor. Both require each other's help. Those who can afford can hire labour for their farms whereas many of the people do *əshə̀ʔə̀ sénsə́ ghə́* 'collective work'. Generally the people show concern for one another and cooperate in many aspects of life including work, celebration and mourning. In a majority of cases people do not need invitations to be part of an activity and the hosts are usually pleased when more people turn up just because they heard about an event from neighbours or other villagers and then decided to participate. In the case of farm work, people are invited to participate. Collectivism in Kejom Ketinguh is evident in several aspects of life including farming, marriage, and death celebration.

3.3.1 Collectivism in Farming

As stated above, collective work is commonly practised by Kejom farmers. This organized form of work is exercised at different levels depending on the number of people as well as their affinities. This is so because working together requires mutual respect, confidence and a good relationship between the people of the group. As few as two people, who could be family members or friends, can work together, taking turns to go to the farm of each one of them.

There could also be groups of three or more people either at the level of quarters or churches (especially among members of Baptist Churches).This type of collective work is also done in a rotating manner so that each day is allocated to work in the farm of one farmer. It is a well-planned activity and the person receiving the group prepares food for the others. In most cases only the staple food, fufucorn and njamanjama is prepared. Where male farmers are involved the food is usually accompanied by palm wine. The other group members could support the host with food items such as boiled corn and groundnuts or fruit such as banana that could be eaten by everyone. In well-organized cases the group members insist on a contribution of agreed amounts of money which are kept in the group's account and which can subsequently be used for other development projects.

3.3.2 Cultivating the Fon's Farm

The Fon's farm is cultivated through collective work. The collectivism in this case is peculiar because it is not rotary. The whole community is obliged to work on the Fon's farm on a particular day. In some cases the community is divided into groups to take care of the different farms located at the palace itself, at Techuh, Mbuandoboh and at Mendongmbo. In this way people from Chua, Ketieh, Timinshui and Chuku work at Mbuandoboh, while those from Tingeh work at Mendongmbo and those from Ntehkezoin, Tiku and Techu work at Techu. The farm around the palace is taken care of by residents of Ntehloh, Kenkung, Mbuaten, Tuaoloh, Buh and others who do not belong to the above mentioned quarters. It is usually very interesting to find thousands of adults gather to work in those farms, especially because of the singing and collectivism on such occasions. The farms are usually cultivated on a day after the country Sunday, called *ǝzhíŋ* '4th weekday'. No one is allowed to work on their farm on this day and defaulters are asked to pay fines or to work alone. The coordination is done by leaders of women's groups in the quarters who inform the rest of the communities by special signals called '*ǝlyúʔ*'. The signals are echoed first in the evening' wúlúǝ, wúlúǝ, wúlúə....... Early in the morning the echoes get people out of bed and accompany them to the farms. These signals are also used as greetings by the different people and groups that come to the farm. The response is the same and work keeps on going. Each person comes along with some snacks but the main meal comes from the palace. Some interesting songs that accompany the work throughout the day are the following.

Song 1
ŋkúnyàm yì á ghə́ kó lú ŋgàʔə̀,
ghə̀ŋ shìʔə̀ á túbɔ́ʔ ə́ ŋkúnyàm djừ gàʔ lá ghɔ̀? wúlúə́, wúlúə́
ŋkúnyàm yì á ghə́ kó lú ŋgàʔə̀,
ghə̀ŋ shìʔə̀ á túbɔ́ʔ ə́ ŋkúnyàm djừ gàʔ lá ghɔ̀? wúlúə́, wúlúə́
'A pig never speaks,
What are you taking the pig to the Tubah court to go and say?
A pig never speaks,
What are you taking the pig to the Tubah court to go and say?'.

Song 2
ó yèsə́ lù vətìʔ və́ nsé sə̀ ghò nsé shèʔà,
yèsə́ lù vətìʔ və́ nsé ó sə̀ ghò nsé shèʔà. wúlúə́, wúlúə́...
ó yèsə́ lù vətìʔ və́ nsé sə̀ ghò nsé shèʔà,
yèsə́ lù vətìʔ və́ nsé ó sə̀ ghò nsé shèʔà. wúlúə́, wúlúə́...
'We the indigenes do not have land to work,
We the indigenes do not have land to work.
We the indigenes do not have land to work,
We the indigenes do not have land to work'.

Song 3
yèsə́ ghò nsé shèʔà mú à nè wùmbùlúʔ è,
yèsə́ ghò nsé shèʔà mú à nè wùmbùlúʔ è. wúlúə́, wúlúə́...
yèsə́ ghò nsé shèʔà mú à nè wùmbùlúʔ è,
yèsə́ ghò nsé shèʔà mú à nè wùmbùlúʔ è. wúlúə́, wúlúə́...
'We do not have land to work because of a Mbororo man,

We do not have land to work because of a Mbororo man.
We do not have land to work because of a Mbororo man,
We do not have land to work because of a Mbororo man'.

Song 4
yèsɔ́ yén lí ntɔ̀n yì à mú à nè wùmbùlúʔ è,
yèsɔ́ yén lí ntɔ̀n yì à mú à nè wùmbùlúʔ è. wúlúɔ́, wúlúɔ́...
yèsɔ́ yén lí ntɔ̀n yì à mú à nè gánákɔ̀ʔ è,
yèsɔ́ yén lí ntɔ̀n yì à mú à nè gánákɔ̀ʔ è. wúlúɔ́, wúlúɔ́...
'We have seen the pot because of a Mbororo man,
We have seen the pot because of a Mbororo man.
We have seen the pot because of a herdsman,
We have seen the pot because of a herdsman'.

Song 5
lá yèsɔ́ zén lí mɔ̀nsò à dìʔ mɔ̀ ɔ̀lɔ́ʔ mpfèn à, à gháʔ ndɔ́ fá fɛ́ ló kɔ́ shìʔɔ̀ á wénɔ́ kɔ̀chú à,
yèsɔ́ zén lí mɔ̀nsò à dìʔ mɔ̀ ɔ̀lɔ́ʔ mpfèn à, à gháʔ ndɔ́ fá fɛ́ ló kɔ́ shìʔɔ̀ á wénɔ́ kɔ̀chú à .wúlúɔ́, wúlúɔ́...
lá yèsɔ́ zén lí mɔ̀nsò à dìʔ mɔ̀ ɔ̀lɔ́ʔ mpfèn à, à gháʔ ndɔ́ fá fɛ́ ló kɔ́ shìʔɔ̀ á wénɔ́ kɔ̀chú à,
yèsɔ́ zén lí mɔ̀nsò à dìʔ mɔ̀ ɔ̀lɔ́ʔ mpfèn à, à gháʔ ndɔ́ fá fɛ́ ló kɔ́ shìʔɔ̀ á wénɔ́ kɔ̀chú à. wúlúɔ́, wúlúɔ́...
'We have bought witchcraft for the entire village and whoever participates will bear the consequences,
We have bought witchcraft for the entire village and whoever participates will bear the consequences.
We have bought witchcraft for the entire village and whoever participates will bear the consequences,
We have bought witchcraft for the entire village and whoever participates will bear the consequences'.

It can be observed that the songs centre around conflicts between farmers and graziers. The first song reflects conflict between a farmer and a grazier of Kejom origin whose pig(s) have destroyed the crops of the former and who takes the matter to court but the court has ruled in favour of the grazier claiming that it cannot obtain information from the pig that does not speak, evidently because the pig owner has corrupted the court. The song shows the desperation of the poor farmer faced with such powerful people in the society. The second, third and fourth songs relate situations of conflict between Kejom farmers and Mbororo cattle rearers. Through the songs, they move back in history to the period when these settlers arrived the village and their cattle caused rampant destruction on crops until the *fǝmbwìn* 'female secret group' had to wage war against the Mbororo and stand their grounds to save their farms and farm land which were gradually being transformed into grazing land. The women spent several days and nights over several weeks protesting until the Mbororo retreated. Song number four narrates a situation where the women who had spent the night outside could see someone who woke up early in the morning and was cooking at home while the women were still in the fields protesting.

The fifth song addresses one of the common ills of the Kejom Ketinguh society, namely, witchraft and seeks to discourage those who could want to get involved.

On their way back home from work in the Fon's farm any young girl they meet is oiled with palm oil in order to enhance her fertility. During the planting season the first farms to be planted are those of the Fon. After doing so, each participant goes home with sample seeds of maize, beans and groundnuts. These samples are mixed up with the individual farmer's seeds in order to also receive the blessings that are in the Fon's seeds. It is necessary to note that the situation described here has evolved considerably as modernity and other realities have come to disrupt the social cohesion that existed in the past. It has become more and more difficult to convince people to work collectively on the Fon's farm such that only part of the village easily responds to the call when it comes for people to go out for the activity.

3.3.3 Collectivism during the Construction of Houses

Farmers in Kejom usually solicit the help of each other in constructing their houses. This assistance can be at any stage of the construction. It could be digging and laying the foundation, fabricating bricks, fetching sticks and bamboos, grass for thatching or the thatching itself. It should be noted that constructing a typical traditional house in Kejom Ketinguh requires sticks, bamboos and grass but with modernity many people have abandoned such houses that were usually exposed to fire accidents. Sundry bricks have gradually replaced the sticks and bamboos and the corrugated iron sheets have replaced the grass used for thatching. In this process collective work could be amongst technicians such as bricklayers and carpenters. It is therefore common to find a technicians' house being constructed by some other technicians for no fare except food and drinks provided by the owner of the house. However most farmers who are well to do hire and pay for the labour of the different technicians involved in the construction.

3.3.4 Collectivism during Marriage Ceremonies

Marriage in Kejom is viewed as a union between two families and not two individuals. That is why the girl's family can only carry out serious negotiations with the boy's family rather than with the boy himself. In this way it becomes a community issue. Family, friends, and neighbours of both families get involved in the planning and organization of the traditional wedding. On the day of the wedding itself, the family of the bride prepares fufucorn and njamanjama alongside egusi, apply camwood on the bride and accompany her to the groom's home early in the evening. Before they arrive several people would have gathered at the groom's home, and have been cooking, eating and drinking in celebration. When the bride arrives birth songs are sung and more food and palmwine are served and the bride's family is offered large quantities of food and drinks. Before the bride's family departs, they are given meat and palm oil which is filled in the pot in which they had brought the njamanjama. The following day, the bride's family shares the meat and oil among themselves and their close friends. Collectivism in marriage is also illustrated in the sense that people are not invited to the occasion and anyone is welcome to stop by, eat and drink and then leave when they choose to.

3.3.5 Collectivism during Death Celebration

When someone dies it affects family members, friends and the entire community. Those who come to condole do not usually come empty handed as men bring along palm wine while women come with any kind of food. All of the food and drinks are used to entertain the mourners who assemble to sympathize with the bereaved family. Digging of the grave has never been the affair of the bereaved family. The young men of that quarter where the person dies take charge of this and in return the children, nieces, nephews of the deceased each give a quantity of palm wine and cigarettes to the young people. At the end of it all they are given food and chicken(s)to thank them for the work done.

3.4 Conclusion

This chapter has provided insights into the lifestyle of the Kejom Ketinguh people, taking into consideration the things they do to ensure that they succeed in their everyday activities which evolve around farming. The way the people collaborate and co-exist has also been addressed in this chapter, showing that there is togetherness in most activities carried out in the village. This has led to a situation whereby there is nothing that happens to one person and which affects the person alone. It should be noted that the Kejom people used to end their daily activities by narrating either folktales, riddles, and/or myths. Any other story can also be told at such a time when they have returned home from the fields after working hard all day long. Story-telling took place mostly after they people took their baths, cooked and ate and then went to lie down in their beds. In other words this was nearly the only form of relaxation and entertainment they had. Nowadays story-telling has been replaced by modern information and communication devices such as television sets and mobile phones while the children tend to study their formal school materials rather than listen to their parents or peers. In appendix seven, we provide a number of folktales, riddles and myths

CHAPTER FOUR
FOOD HABITS AND COOKING METHODS

4.0 Introduction
The food habits of farmers of Kejom Ketinguh are very simple. They survive on the variety of crops grown in their fields and occasionally consume wild fruit and vegetables. The varieties of insects they eat include *tǝmbvǝn* 'grasshoppers', *ǝntsì* 'crickets', and *mǝnshìʔ* 'beetles'. Animals such as *vǝndìm* 'rat moles', *mǝbwìn* 'squirrels' *vǝnjù* 'cane rats' and *shúsǝ́* 'fish' are popular alongside cattle, goats and pigs. Many birds such as *mbvúsǝ́* 'chickens', and *tǝ̀tsúʔ* 'partridges' are popular delicacies but the people do not eat nocturnal birds like *ǝ̀mpfìŋ* 'owls' and scavengers like *ǝ̀nghŏnghò* 'crows'. This is related to beliefs the people have about such birds. For example, crows are believed to carry away the fertility of the soil when chased away from the farms with soil rather than using stones or shouting them away. Generally, crows dig out maize seeds once planted or eat the corn itself when it is ready but people are discouraged from sending them away using soil. The owl on its part is believed to be a messenger of *vǝ̀zhí* 'witches' and 'wizards', and it is advisable to burn it to ashes when caught.

Kǝ̀báyn 'fufucorn' and *mbàsǝ̀ ǝ́ pfíʔǝ́* 'njamanjama' is the staple food that Kejom people eat on a regular basis. No matter what they eat, if they go on for more than a day without having this staple food they will begin to complain about starvation. Recently, delicacies such as rice which was eaten only on Christmas days is now eaten on ordinary days in most homes in the village.

4.1 Method of Preparing *Kǝ̀báyn* 'fufucorn' and *Mbàsǝ̀ ǝ́ Pfíʔǝ́* 'njamanjama'
In order to prepare the Kejom staple food, *kǝ̀báyn* the following items are needed:

- kɜbáyn 'corn flour'
- múɜ 'water'
- ntòyn 'a pot'
- kyé? 'sort of tray'
- ɜkóŋ ɔ́ kɜbáyn, 'fufucorn pestle'
- tɜfú 'banana/plantain leaves'
- kɜbòlɜ 'calabash'
- tsèkèlè? 'sieve'
- ŋkímɜ 'saucer'

The corn flour is obtained from the harvested maize that is stored at ɜkáŋ 'kitchen barn'. The corn is husked, removed from the cobs and taken to a grinding platform which can be ɜtí 'grinding stone', mechanical grinding mill and more recently diesel/petrol mills, as well as electrical mills. This process leads one to obtain the flour needed for the preparation of fufucorn.

A quantity of water is put into a pot and placed on the three-stone fire place. While water is being allowed to boil flour is sifted into the kyé? 'tray'. When the water boils, a certain quantity of it is extracted and stored in another pot or dish that can keep it warm until the end of the cooking process. A small quantity of the sifted flour is mixed with cold water inside the kɜbòlɜ 'calabash' and mixed up with the boiling water standing on the fireplace. It is stirred up to have a smooth mixture using the ɜkóŋ ɔ́ kɜbáyn 'fufucorn pestle'. It is then left to boil for some few minutes, after which the rest of the sieved flour is poured into this mixture and the stirring process resumes. It is stirred continually to obtain a smooth mixture and water is added progressively depending on how hard the mixture is. After stirring for a while another quantity of water is added and the mixture is allowed to boil for some more minutes. This process is called ɔ́pfè ɔ́ kɜbáyn 'cooking fufucorn'. After this time there is a final stirring to completely have a smooth and well-cooked mixture. The *ŋkímə̀* 'saucer' is then used to dish out certain quantities and rounded up either inside the *kə̀bòlə̀* 'calabash' or wrapped on leaves into loaves call *tə̀ghíftə́ kə̀báyn* 'fufucorn loaves'.

In removing the fufucorn from the pot, the husband's *kyéʔ* 'plate/tray' is served first, followed by that of other members of the household and that which is to be stored for the next meal is kept in another *kyéʔ* and covered with banana leaves. The fufucorn is served with *mbàsə̀ ə́ pfíʔə́* 'njamanjama' which had been prepared earlier.

To prepare the *mbàsə̀ ə́ pfíʔə́* the following items are required.
- *mbàsə̀ ə́ pfíʔə́* 'njamanjama'
- *fə̀mbváŋ* 'salt'
- *mə̀nzhíʔ* 'oil'
- *ŋgə̀ʔsə́* 'egusi'

The njamanjama is selected, washed and part of it is put inside a pot on the three-stone fire place. The egusi is mixed with a small quantity of water inside the *kə̀bòlə̀* 'calabash' and spoon full sizes are placed on top of the vegetable in the pot before adding the rest of the njamanjama. The mixture is then allowed to boil for a while after which it is turned upside down in the pot to permit it to get ready evenly. Salt and palm oil are added and allowed to boil for a short time and then everything is stirred up in order to obtain a tasteful mixture. The fufucorn and njamanjama can be served hot, warm or even cold and eaten at any moment of the day as breakfast, lunch or supper.

4.2 Cassava and it Derivatives
Cassava is among the tubers that is most consumed in Kejom Ketinguh, only next to maize. It is consumed in different forms ranging from just boiling the cassava and eating to processing it into other products.

The boiled cassava can be consumed alone, with avocado, beans or pounded together with beans. Flour made from cassava can also be prepared as fufucassava and consumed with any vegetable. Derivatives from cassava include *tapioca*, *menyondo* and *makala*.

In order to obtain *tapioca*, the cassava is harvested, peeled, washed and graded either using a hand grater or a machine. The paste is put into a bag and tied between sticks in order to drain out the excessive starch. After 2-3days when the paste has almost completely dried up, it is put into a basin and the loams are softened with hands. The smoothened paste is dry-fried in a big frying pan. The *tapioca* can be white if no palm oil is added or yellowish if palm oil is added. The *tapioca* can be consumed by soaking in fresh water and eaten with avocado, sugar or peanuts. It can also be prepared as fufu in boiled water.

Menyondo on its part is prepared by soaking peeled cassava into water for some days until it ferments. When the cassava ferments and gets soft, it is taken out, washed and the root-like particles extracted. The rest is pressed together to extract the water from it and then it is ground into a paste either on a grinding stone or on a mill. The smooth paste is again mixed up with clean water and certain quantities are tied on banana leaves with the aid of ropes from the banana stem. The bundles are then boiled. Once ready it can be eaten with avocado, peanut paste or any vegetable.

Photo 4: *Menyondo* Packaged for Sale

Menyondo is a common cash product of the people of Kejom especially those of the lower part of the village where cassava is grown in large quantities. Three of them are sold in the village for 100FCFA and it stands out as one of the Kejom products that is widely consumed in many parts of the Cameroon.

Makala on it part is prepared at the start just like *tapioca* but the paste in the bag is not allowed for days as keeping it only for one day is sufficient. Early in the morning the bag is untied, the cassava paste is poured into a mortar and pounded together with ripe banana to obtain a homogeneous mixture. A quantity of salt is added to taste and the mixture is then shaped with hands into smaller balls and deep fried in bleached palm oil. It is also very popular and mostly sold only locally.

4.3   Preparation of *Nkáŋ* 'corn beer'
Nkáŋ 'corn beer' remains one of the most popular drinks among the Kejom Ketinguh people next to palmwine. These

are the two kinds of alcoholic drinks produced locally and in large quantities. They are also the ones that are used during ceremonies. In order to prepare the corn beer, a quantity of corn is soaked in water for at least three days after which it is taken out of water and put in a bag or covered with plantain/banana leaves for it to sprout. The germinated seeds are then dried in the sun and milled into flour. The flour is mixed in a carefully measured quantity of water and boiled for close to 3 hours. It is taken off from the fire, kept in a cold place and later put through a sieve to separate the chaffs from the liquid. At this stage the liquid obtained is sweet although the degree of sweetness depends on the degree of fermentation that took place. After one or two days of fermentation the liquid becomes alcoholic. During ceremonies both varieties of fermented and unfermented corn beer are usually served on choice of the one drinking.

4.4   Conclusion
The kinds of food eaten by the Kejom Ketinguh people are presented in this chapter alongside the methods of preparation. It shows the people depend mostly on maize and cassava but minimally on the other crops they produce for their food.

CHAPTER FIVE
CROP CULTIVATION

5.0   Introduction

As mentioned earlier, more than 90% of the total population is involved in crop cultivation. The activities take different forms depending on the proximity of farmlands to the main settlements, soil fertility, relief and population pressure. The methods of cultivation used on the arable lands include intensive cultivation with enclosures (practised mostly in the vicinity of homesteads), annual crop land with short fallow (in densely populated areas), annual crop land with long fallow (in averagely dense and less dense areas), and permanent fields (1,250-1,300m), medium altitude (1,300-1,799m) and high altitude (1,799-2,400m) are common with different crops grown thus giving the village a diversified agricultural base. After presenting the farming system which includes the inputs, processes and outputs (crops) the cultivation of the different crops will then be discussed in detail. The following table illustrates the Kejom Ketinguh farming system.

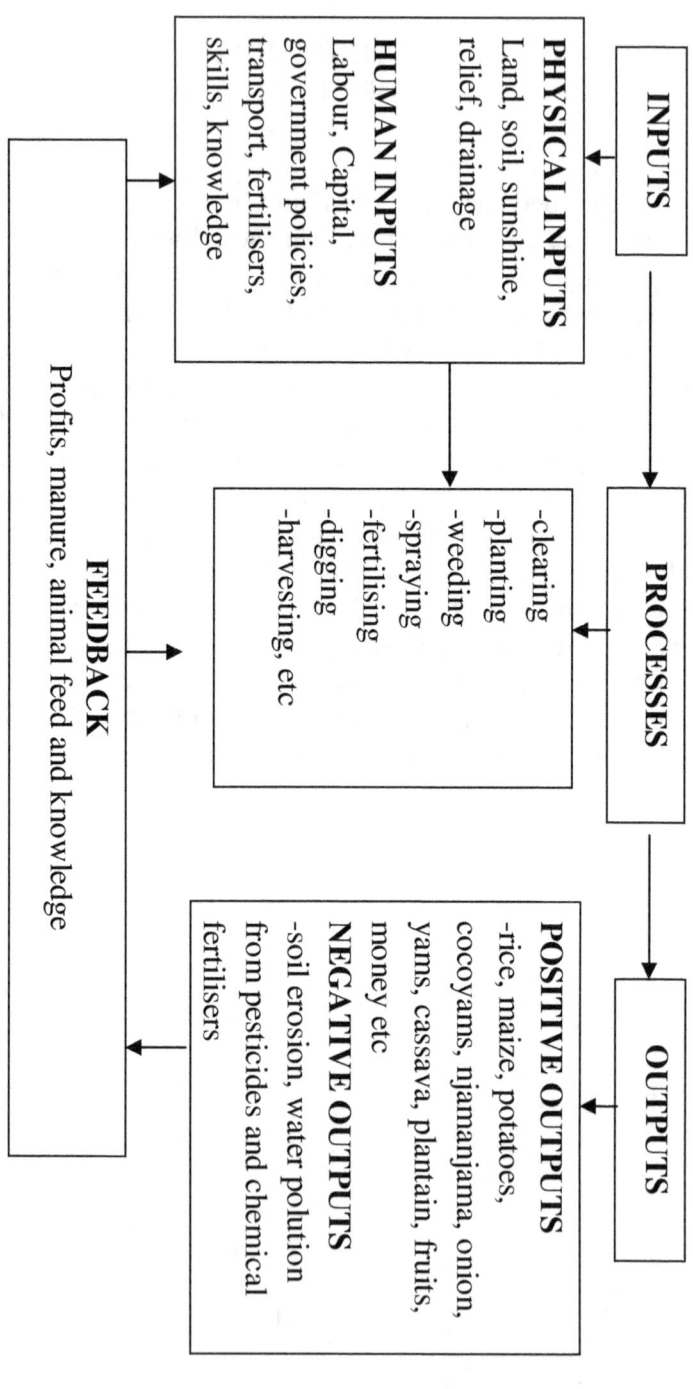

Figure 4: Farming as a System in Kejom Ketinguh
Source: Adapted from Fellmann, Getis & Getis (1997)

The inputs that go into the farming process are from natural and human origin. They include the land, labour, capital and skills. The farmers then put into value the resources through processes such as clearing, sowing, and harvesting of the crops. The processes can give rise either to positive or negative outputs such as having the finished products and money gained from the sale of the products and waste products and soil erosion respectively.

Feedback is what is put back into the system. The main two examples in Kejom Ketinguh are the money from the sale of the outputs and the knowledge gained from the whole manufacturing process. This knowledge could then be used to make the product better or improve the efficiency of the processes subsequently.

Type	Kejom Name
maize	àsáŋ
cassava	kàsá
colocasia(Taro)	ə̀làŋ ə́káʔə́ káʔə́
beans	àkwɛ́n
yams	àlɛ́m
cocoyams	ə̀làŋ ə́ mə̀ŋkáʔə́
bananas/plantains	tə̀ŋgɔ̀m
arabica coffee	Kòfí
groundnut	bə́lə̀ŋ
pumpkins	àbúʔ
potatoes	ndɔ̀ŋ ə́ mə̀ŋkáʔə́
soya beans	sòyà bíns
avocado	byə́
sweet potatoes	ndɔ̀ŋ ə́ lyìmə́
raffia palms	àlyùʔ
paddy rice	àkwɛ́n ə́ mə̀ŋkáʔə́
njamanjama	mbàsə̀ ə́ pfíʔə́

onion	ànyɔ̀s
tomatoes	fɘnyɔ́ʔ fɘ́ mɘ̀ŋkáʔɘ̀
Garlics	gálìk
Carrot	kárɔ̀t

Table 5: Main Crops Cultivated in Kejom Ketinguh
Source: Field Observation, 2014

The crops cultivated can be valued by observing the surface area and the annual production of some major crops as shown on table 6.

Crop type	Area cultivated (hectares)	Quantity/hectare (tons)	Annual production (tons)
maize	200	1.5	700
beans	200	1.2	640
cassava	100	25	2,500
yams	95	20	1,900
sweet potatoes	75	25	1,875
plantain	120	30	2,600
tomatoes	-	500-1,000kg	200
njamanjama	-	-	2,500
pepper	-	-	0.4
spices	-		0.6
coffee	-	90kg	0.8
potatoes			1,500

Table 6: Some Major Crop Types in Kejom Ketinguh, Surface Area Covered and Annual Production
Source: Tubah Sub-Divisional Delegation of Agriculture (2009)

The crops are grown in diverse forms and include mixed cropping, sole cropping, crop rotation with the use of diverse techniques such as slash and burn, slash and mulch, rotational bush fallow and shifting cultivation. Although some techniques have changed because of population increase and technological development, others have remained the same over the years as shall be shown subsequently.

The different categories of crops presented in table 6 are further discussed in the following sub sections.

5.1 Cereals and legumes

The cereals and legumes shown in table 6 include maize, beans, soya beans, groundnuts and pumpkins. They need physically good soils rich in humus which the village provides. They thrive in low, medium and high altitudes. Maize occupies the first position in term of surface area cultivated. Due to mixed farming beans is cultivated alongside maize and so occupies a similar surface area cultivated.

Photo 5: Mixed Farm at Kumendongmbo

The photograph shows a maize farm at Kumendongmbo[4] where potatoes, and carrots are also grown albeit out of the

---

[4]This forest area is far away from the settlement part of the village and close to the neigbouring Kejom Keku village.

normal season. It is necessary to note that the fresh maize shown in this photograph in the month of April were planted in February in the heart of the dry season. It is due to enhanced irrigation schemes that such cultivation is possible. Due to improved irrigation, the cultivation of some crops in some parts of Kejom Ketinguh is possible throughout the year. At the time the photograph was taken in April the carrots, also planted in February were already being harvested, while the potatoes were expected to be harvested the following month (May) and the maize later in June.

Mixed farming is also commonly practised during the normal planting season which takes place between March and April.

Photo 6: A Mixed Farm in Chua Quarter

The farm in this photograph unlike the one in photograph 5 is a farm planted in the later part of March. The crops here are therefore normal rainy season crops depending on natural rainfall and sunshine conditions. The photograph was taken in June at a time when the maize was already flowering and the beans is mature and being harvested. The maize will be harvested only in August and in this part of the village the next maize planting season will be only in March the following year.

Photo 7: Maize, Pumpkins and Colocasia Grown on the Same Farm

This photograph was taken in August when corn had just been harvested from the farm. The pumpkins are already mature and just have to be taken home. The colocasia is still to completely mature. What is of interest is the fact that all of these items had been planted at the beginning of the planting season in March in the same farm.

Photo 8: Sweet Potatoes and Potatoes Planted on Separate Sections of the Same Ridges

The photograph also taken in August shows a mixed farm where items that cannot be planted together are planted on the same ridge next to each other. Interestingly the farmer consistently plants sweet potatoes on one part of the ridge and potatoes on the other.

5.2 Tubers
The tubers in table 6 include yams, cassava, potatoes, colocasia and cocoyams. They are both grown by men and women but the male dominate in the production of yams. Cassava is cultivated on a larger surface area than all the other tubers. Next to it are yams and the different species include yellow yams, sweet yams, white yams and aerial yams. These are followed by potatoes, colocasia, sweet potatoes, and cocoyams, in that order.

5.2.1 Cassava

This crop is mostly grown on gentle slopes of 1,400 to 1,600m and the alluvial soils of Tikebeng. The annual output for cassava in 2013 was estimated at about 2,400 tons (Velem, 2013). As discussed earlier cassava derivatives include tapioca, menyondo, makala, etc. which are found in the different markets.

Plate 1: Cassava and Tapioca

Photograph A shows the cassava tubers which can either be consumed by just boiling or can be transformed into other products. Photograph B, shows one of the products, tapioca which is widely consumed in and out of the village.

5.2.2 Potatoes

This is a starchy, tuberous crop with different species and colours. It is one of the crops in the village produced in very large quantities after maize and cassava. The crop originated from the lowlands of south-central Chile in South America and is commonly called 'Irish potato'.

Photo 9: Potato Farm

Photograph 9 shows a large potato farm at Chuku planted in the month of January and watered by running pipes. Due to the advances in irrigation schemes the potatoes here will be ready for consumption and commercialization during the month of May.

Photo10: Potatoes Packaged in Bags

Photograph 7 shows a portion of the Chuku market where potatoes and several food crops are sold. The price ranges from 2,000FCFA per bucket during peak harvest periods to about 4,000FCFA when the product becomes scarce.

5.3   Market garden crops
In Kejom Ketinguh, big gardens have been established by some young men who produce mostly for commercialization. They apply fertilizers, cow dung, fowl droppings and other forms of natural manure to enrich the soil. Vegetables such as lettuce, onions, carrots, cabbages, and more significantly the *njamanjama* are grown.

5.3.1   Njamanjama
This is the most important of the market gardening crops grown in Kejom. According to Velem (2013), about 2,100 bags of this vegetable are produced a week. The crop is grown throughout the year and everywhere particularly in the upper plateau of Kwighe. The main system of cultivation is the night paddocking system peculiar only to this area in the North West

region. The crop grows in abundance here because of the availability of manure, the rich volcanic soils, fowl and other animal droppings and the high demand both at home as a stable food crop and in urban centres such as Bamenda, Yaoundé and Douala as a popular vegetable.

Plate 2: Njamanjama

In plate 2, photograph A shows ready-to-harvest njamanjama while B shows the one that has already been harvested. It should be noted that harvesting is done in many sequences due to the fact that it takes only about 1-2 weeks after a harvest for the vegetable to grow and be ready for another harvest. A farmer can harvest up to 5 times before the njamanjama plant expires and stops producing fresh leaves.

5.3.2 Leeks

In recent years, the cultivation of leeks has gradually gained grounds in this area. According to Joseph Vitsuh, head of a farmer's common initiative group (personal communication), a minimum of 1,000 packets are harvested each day. Each packet weighs between 5 and 10kg. The quantity produced is determined by the seasonal variations in rainfall.

5.3.3 Tomatoes

Tomatoes is one of the widely grown market garden crops of this village which thrives in the well-drained areas of Kwighe. It is mostly grown by young strong and dynamic people since it requires constant care by way of spraying against pests and continuous daily harvesting of ripe fruit at the appropriate time.

Photo 11: Baskets of Tomatoes

The photograph shows baskets of tomatoes displayed in the Kyephen market for sale. Transportation is easy and safe on such ǝkjè 'baskets' made out of material from raffia palms.

5.3.4 Onion

Onion is also one of the most widely grown market garden crops especially on the hilly sites. According to Velem (2013) its production amounts to about 2,400 buckets (15 litres each) per week.

Plate 3: Onion Farm and Harvested Onion

As one of the major cash crops of the village many farmers have gradually abandoned food crop production to the cultivation of onion which can easily fetch them money and improve on their standards of living. Some of the common species are tiezier, panar, and tropica.

5.3.5 Other crops

Other market crops produced in this village in significant quantities include carrots, garlics, and cabbages. Large quantities are harvested and exported each week during the harvesting season. They are produced almost all year round especially with the irrigation schemes in place.

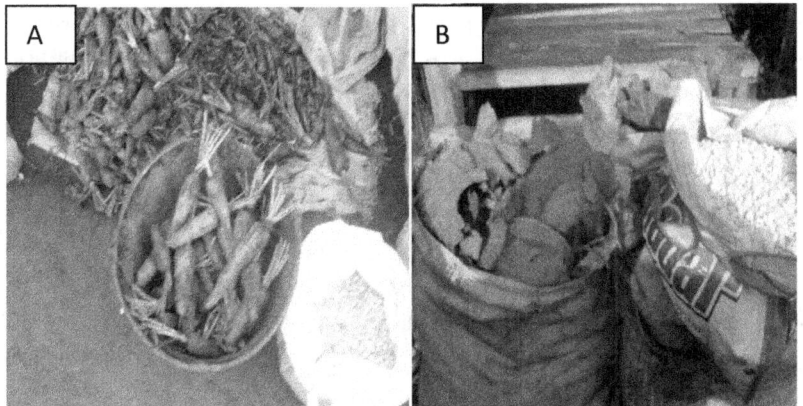

Plate 4: Carrots and Cabbages Displayed at the Chuku Market

The plate shows carrots (A) and cabbages (B) which are some of the highly cultivated vegetables in the village.

5.4 Perennial crops
These are crops that take a long time, at least a year, to get mature and start producing. They include coffee, bananas, plantains, and raffia palms.

5.4.1 coffee
The coffee plant enjoys permanent land rights in Kejom Ketinguh. It grows in all altitudes and occupies a surface area of approximately 420 hectares. Coffee normally belongs to men and constituted the base of agricultural take off in the village. The species grown here is called arabica coffee. Today, however, it is grown in very negligible quantities because of the fall of its price in the international market.

5.4.2 Bananas and Plantains
Nearly all settlements are surrounded by both banana and plantain trees. While some are sold in the local markets, the people tend to consume them more and more. The bananas

could either be cooked unripe or allowed to ripen before eating. It is mostly the ripe bananas that are sold in markets. Plantains are more frequent in the markets than bananas although still in little quantities.

5.4.3 Raffia Palm

This crop is quite old in the village and acts as a means of land security providing materials for construction as well as a source of income. Naturally, it grows well in hydromorphic soils normally found along rivers and streams. It constitutes part of the gallery forest. It is grown and exploited mostly by men and has a gestation period of 15 years. Planting usually takes place during the rainy season since the plant requires much water to grow. Throughout its life span, only trimming, and cleaning is done as far as care for the plant is concerned. The wine tapped from raffia is very important for the people and they use it for their traditional ceremonies.

Photo 12: Raffia bush

The photograph displays portions of a raffia bush in the village. Apart from tapping of palm wine from such bushes, it is equally a source of raw material for handicraft works such as weaving bags, making baskets, beds, beehives, etc. It is equally a construction material for traditional houses and above all a watershed for most springs in the community.

5.4.4 Rice

Rice is grown in the lowlands of Kejom Ketinguh as part of the Upper Noun Valley Development Authority (UNVDA) programme. The rice fields occupy swampy farming zones of Techuh quarter, supplied by extensions of the Bamendjin dam. The common type of rice cultivated here is paddy. According to the chief of post for agriculture for Kejom Ketinguh (Personal Communication), about 25 hectares of land are under rice cultivation. Yields per hectare stand at about 20 tons and the annual production is evaluated at about 500 tons.

To sum up this chapter on the different crops cultivated in Kejom Ketinguh, the statistics in table 7 have been provided to show annual production in 2000 and 2012.

Number	Type of crop	Production in tons (2000)	Production in tons (2012)
1	maize	1,000	1,500
2	beans	500	500
3	groundnuts	50	55
4	cassava	2,000	2,400
5	potatoes	2,000	2,300
6	njamanjama	3,000	5,040
7	leeks	150	3,600
8	carrots	-	260
9	onion	200	500
10	paddy rice	900	800

Table 7: Annual Output of Crops in Kejom Ketinguh in 2000 and 2012
Source: Velem (2013)

The table indicates that there was a slight increase in the quantity of most crops produced within those ten years. There was a remarkable increase in the quantities of njamanjama and leeks due to the fact that many farmers adopted the night paddock manuring system. This was encouraged by NGOs such as CIPCRE and INADES Formation. Another reason is the increased cooperation between farmers and graziers and high demand of the products in the market.

Rice production has dropped from about 900 tons to 800. This drop in tonnage is due to the collapse and poor rehabilitation of the Techuh dam supplying water to the rice fields. However reconstruction work on the dam has been going on since the beginning of 2014.

5.5 Conclusion

The focus in this chapter has been on the crops cultivated in this village. They range from cereals and legumes to tubers, market gardening and perennial crops. It is also shown in this chapter that mixed farming is common in this area and that some market gardening crops can be cultivated all year round.

CHAPTER SIX
FARMING SYSTEMS

6.0 Introduction
Farming in Kejom Ketinguh is done using different systems of cultivation. These systems vary from one agricultural zone of the village to another. In this chapter the most popular farming methods used by the people are discussed and the stages involved in the farming cycle are also presented.

6.1.1 Slash and Burn
This method is mostly used on slopes whose gradient is greater than 10% and which are covered by forests. It is done at the Mendongmbo forest area, which is a major farming zone in Kejom Ketinguh. During the dry season the prospected farm lands are cleared and debris are allowed to dry for a few weeks. Later they are set on fire to prepare the plot for planting. In other areas of the village the practice has been reduced to what is commonly termed *mfwĭ* 'ankara'. Here the bush is cleared using machetes and hoes. The cleared grass is then arranged into furrows, covered with soil and then fire is set on them. When the rainy season begins, crops are planted on the burnt ridges which become reddish in colour with the first rain. Yields are very high when the ankara are prepared during the first year but they drastically drop in the subsequent years.

6.1.2 Slash and Mulch
This is a sustainable form of agriculture which is rapidly gaining grounds in the village. It is a system of cultivation by which grass is cut down, left to dry up and then it is gathered into furrows. The grass is then covered with soil and arranged into ridges. It causes very little damage to the environment and makes significant improvement to agriculture. It is an

alternative source of fertilizers as the decaying grass provide organic matter to the soil. This system is practised all over the village.

6.1.3 Shifting Cultivation

This is an old and primitive method of subsistent farming that was once carried out in Kejom Ketinguh. It involved the clearing and cultivation of a piece of land for a short period of time. When the soil lost its fertility and yields dropped, the farmland was abandoned for a couple of years to regain its fertility. This shifting cultivation involved not only the shifting from one farm land to another but also the displacement of the family. This system was popular because agriculture was mainly done in a traditional manner without any modern facilities such as fertilizers. The degree to which soil fertility was usually regained depended on the extent of the fallow period. Soil humus increased as a result of fallen litter so that this was a cheap system for subsistent farmers as it did not require fertilizers or more sophisticated means of cultivation. However, with increase in population, there is pressure on land and such a system cannot continue to survive.

6.1.4 Bush Fallowing

This is an improved system of shifting cultivation in Kejom Ketinguh today. It is a method of farming whereby farmers tend to rotate their farm as yields decrease with years. When this happens, the plot is abandoned for thick vegetation to grow in it so that it can regain its fertility. The farmers abandon it for the next plot and only return to it after some years when the plot must have regained its fertility. Here, cultivation rotates on a fixed area of farmland while settlement is permanent. It is very common at Kwighe where the volcanic soils gradually lose fertility due to erosion. Recently in this area, it has been difficult to allow plots to fallow for long due to land scarcity.

6.1.5 Night Paddock Manuring System

This system is commonly used in cultivating market gardening crops at the upper plateau of the village. It is carried out in the stages presented below.

The first stage involves the making of a cattle pen on a delimited area of any length or width, depending on the famer's ability and input. Cattle are brought in to spend nights in the pen for a period of two to three months, depending on the size of the pen and the number of cattle. Most often, this first stage takes place between November and March as the farmers prepare for the planting season. With irrigation techniques it no longer matters when market gardening crops are cultivated in the village. In the mornings, the cattle are moved to the hill slopes for grazing and then brought back into the pen in the evening. The herdsmen stay besides the pen in well-constructed huts to protect the cattle from thieves. The urine and dung released by the cattle produce the manure used for cultivation.

Plate 5: Cattle Pens with and without Cattle

Photograph A shows cattle in the pen. They spend the night in the pen, urinate and excrete on the plot which is what adds to the fertility of the soil. During the day, the cattle go out and eat grass. Photo B shows a cattle pen that cattle have just left, pending tilling and formation of ridges for cultivation of either njamanjama, onions, cabbages or tomatoes. The choice is at the discretion of the farmer.

The second stage involves the tilling of the soil, for the formation of ridges and planting. In the case of njamanjama it takes about 2-4 weeks after planting for the njamanjama to germinate, grow and begin producing leaves.

The third stage involves weeding grass from the njamanjama in order to enable it to grow properly. Usually weeding goes on simultaneously with harvesting which can take place five or six times depending on the maintenance. The second, third and fourth harvests are usually the peak. A bag of njamanjama weighs about 40kg.

In some situations, the cattle pen is just prepared and sold to someone else to cultivate. The person who buys loses rights over the piece of land after harvesting.

6.1.6 Intensive Rice Farming

The field is cleared and tilled with the aid of trained cattle while in some cases tilling is done with the use of tractors. The latter case is common with farmers who have grouped themselves into the Techuh Rice Union. They apply for tractors, seed and other farm inputs from the UNVDA. Cultivation is done under the supervision of its extension workers. After tilling, the rice fields are softened and rice from the nurseries is planted manually. In the dry season the rice is harvested and the fields prepared for food crops in the rainy season. Table 8 indicates the different stages involved in rice cultivation at Techuh in Kejom Ketinguh.

Stages	Period
Land preparation and seed germination in nurseries.	between July and August
Transplanting and fertilization of the fields.	September to November
Rice matures and is ready for harvesting, rice stalks cleared and burnt.	November to February
Fields are bare and exposed awaiting the cultivation of food crops.	February to March

Table 8 : Steps Involved in Rice Cultivation
Source: Adopted from Velem (2013)

According to the chief of the Kejom Ketinguh agricultural post (Personal Communication), the yields per hectare stand at about 20 to 25 tons.

6.1.8 Crop Rotation

Crop rotation with regards to organic farming involves changing the type of crop grown in one area on regular basis. Organic farmers usually plant alternate groups of plants (roots, cereals, legumes, etc) in order to enhance the fertility of the soil and prevent pests and diseases from building up. Crop rotation is practised both in the upper plateau of Kwighe and the plains of Tikebeng. In the upper plateau it is practised on the paddocks, after harvesting vegetables. The vegetables are usually rotated with food crops such as maize, beans and potatoes.

In the plains, crop rotation is practised at Techuh where paddy rice is cultivated. After harvesting of rice in the month of February and March, the rice stalks are cleared, burnt and the fields prepared for the cultivation of food crops such as maize, vegetables and beans amongst others.

6.1.9 Fruit cultivation

In Kejom Ketinguh, there is no intensive cultivation of fruit. Fruit trees are dotted here and there around the compound and in other far off farms. Most of the fruit trees found around homes also serve as wind brakes. Such fruit include bananas, avocados, mangoes, papayas, guavas, pineapple, shea butter nuts, plums, etc. It is rare to find a whole farm dedicated for the cultivation of fruit.

Apart from these domesticated fruit, wild fruit are equally part of the diet of the Kejom people. They are found in the transition area between the plains and upper plateau called Kechetang, and the bush area between the village and Balikumbat called Bambyeh. Some of these fruit are *dzè, kòsàkàlyù?, kònywì?tò, kòntsù?* and *kòmbámbáyn* some of which are found mostly in raffia bushes or around water courses.

Plate 6: Some Wild Fruit in Kejom Ketinguh

Photograph A shows some fruit on the *kòsàkàlyù?* tree and B also shows fruit on the *kòmbámbáyn kó ntàŋ* tree.

6.1.10 Irrigation Farming

In Kejom Ketinguh irrigation farming is visible in the rice fields as well as in the cultivation of market gardening crops. In the rice fields at Techuh water from the dam is directed into rice plots immediately after planting.

Irrigation activities started within farming in Kejom as recently as 1999. In the past, however farmers had started cultivating besides water courses at the heart of the dry season in order to overcome water shortages. Then they used buckets and watering cans to supply water manually especially to their njamanjama and tomato farms.

Plate 7: Irrigation of Farms at Kumendongmbo

As seen on the photographs, the pipes convey water from permanent streams from the forest into the farms. This permits cultivation all year round. Mr. Joseph Vitsuh was the first farmer in Kwighe who introduced a sort of modern irrigation after noticing that the demand for njamanjama was not satisfied during the dry season. Not only was supply insufficient, prices increased enormously. Joseph Vitsuh began by identifying streams that could supply water during the dry season. Depending on the location of the farmers involved, the most appropriate routes were chosen. As the land is prone to erosion, the farmers planted live hedges to stabilize them. When they had to cross a deep gorge or a major water course, they used hollowed-out logs as pipes to link the steep banks. By the year 2000, the system was irrigating more than 10 hectares benefiting some 40 farmers. As many farmers opted for the technique, Mr. Vitsuh conveyed this request to the Indigenous Soil and Water Conservation programme (ISWC), which helped in improving the system and today farmers especially those around Chuku, Kumendonmbo, and Mbuahndoboh no longer depend entirely on the raining season to plant their crops; they plant all year round.

6.2 Stages Involved in Farming
Agriculture is a system that involves inputs, processes and output. Input is used here to refer to both physical (soil fertility and climatic conditions) and human factors (capital, labour and technology). These have been presented above as factors affecting the farming process. The stages involved in farming have been narrowed down in this book to site selection, cutting down grass, sowing and harvesting.

6.2.1 Site Selection
For any meaningful cultivation to take place, the site is first of all chosen. The selection of the site depends on the availability of land. Land in Kejom Ketinguh belongs to the forefathers and the Fon is the custodian of the land. In this way access to land is through inheritance, renting, begging or more recently by buying.
    Family land is inherited and shared by the male children of a particular family. Land is not usually given to the women as they are expected to get married, go to their marital homes and eventually have access to their husband's land.

This act of inheritance gives the man the right to ownership though he might not be the person to exploit and manage the land on a daily basis.

In Kejom Ketinguh it is also possible to beg land. Some people have begged and cultivated land for so many years and after generations they claimed ownership. Those who give out such lands are known to have extensive land surfaces and since they cannot cultivate all of it or because of their generosity, they offer it to those who are willing to work. Generally they do not receive any material compensation from the beggar.

Another way to gain access to land is to hire. People who have the means can rent a field for a season and then return it after harvesting their crops. This is very common on the rice fields of Techuh and market gardening fields of Kwighe where people construct pens and after manuring using the night paddock system, they give them out for others to cultivate.

Furthermore people can have access to land when they buy it. Land can be sold out to fellow villagers and even to foreigners by those who own the land. The price depends on the accessibility of the plot and the fertility of the soil.

Once the land is acquired, the farmer determines the type of crop to cultivate and then sets out to work. Maize farms are fairly distributed in the village but njamanjama and other vegetables usually do well in very fertile areas such as Kumendonmbo and areas of night paddocking found in many parts of the upper plateau where the climate is very suitable for such crops. If it is for rice cultivation, the farmer begins by cutting down the grass but if it is for vegetable cultivation, they first make a cattle pen where the cattle will be kept, and if it is a maize farm, the farmer sets out to cut down the grass or trees.

6.2.2 Clearing of the Fields

After identifying the parcel to be cultivated, the farmers start by clearing the grassland or the forest. This activity can be done by the individual owner or he can invite his friends to assist depending on the size of the plot. Alternatively someone can be paid to do the clearing. This stage of cultivation is almost exclusively done by men using machetes. Clearing is normally done between December and January in preparation for the major planting season and between August and September for the minor planting season of *àsáŋ ɔ́ ŋgwʉ́* 'dry season maize'. If it is a piece of land that has been cultivated previously the clearing is done systematically with grass gathered into furrows, but if it is a new plot with thick vegetation, the grass is kept at random and assembled later. Next is the making of ridges.

6.2.3 Making Ridges

Farms in the village are made up of ridges and furrows arranged in rows. The grass that was cleared previously is arranged in furrows and soil from the old ridges is used to cover the grass to form new ridges where the crops will be planted. The process is done at two stages, *kɔ̀ŋkàs* and *kɔ̀ŋkɔ́m*. That is the first grass covering and the second which is done after spreading njamanjama or beans seeds on the ridges. Maize and other crops are usually planted after the ridge has been completely constructed.

6.2.4 Sowing or Planting

Planting of most crops is done the same day the ridges are made otherwise the soil will become hard and make planting difficult. In the case of maize, planting is done much later when the first rains come and since the soil on the ridges has been hardened people normally use sharp objects such as machetes to bury the maize in the ridges. Mixed planting is very common such that a variety of crops can be found in the same farm. In a maize farm either beans, cassava, potatoes, cocoyams, yams, groundnuts can also be planted. In a njamanjama farm, onions, cabbages, garlics, leeks, and even maize can be planted although sparingly. The principal crop is always given preference in the farm and the others are dotted here and there.

6.2.5 Weeding

Closely related to soil fertility, proper weeding determines proper growth and productivity of crops. In fields where proper weeding is not done, growth of crops is retarded or even damaged by pests from the grass. Weeding concerns all crops and varies in intensity from crop to crop. One reason why farmers cultivate only small plots is the task of weeding; it is tedious due to the speed with which weeds grow and the urgency for them to be uprooted. Generally for maize farms, the weeding is done twice before harvesting. The first weeding is called òsúʔó kòfùʔ and is done more meticulously, while the second weeding, òzáʔsó kòfùʔ is much lighter but sometimes accompanied by mulching depending on the sub crops such as cocoyams, yams, potatoes found in the farm. This permits a better uptake of minerals from the soil. If the field has market gardening crops, the weeding process is more intense and continuous due to the multiple harvests. The least neglect of weeds destroys the quality and affects the quantity of the harvest. Generally the weeds grow faster than the crops and weeding is not only tedious but also poses more health risks because at this time of the year (May-June) there are lots of mosquitoes and other flies due to the rains. Even contact with certain leaves leads to itching and those who have money prefer to hire labour while others still turn to family and friends for help. The farmers use their hands and the hoes for the weeding process. The hoe is used to soften the ground and the grass is picked up with the hands.

6.2.6   Harvesting

This process varies with the crop concerned. There is usually a lot of collective work in harvesting of maize and vegetables. Beans are usually harvested progressively and help is not required. Maize is harvested between August and September while gardening crops are harvested progressively and for so many times before some of the crops finally stop producing.

6.2.7   The Agricultural Calendar

In order to understand the agricultural calendar of Kejom Ketinguh, it is important to note the days of the week (Appendix 2) and months of the year (Appendix 3) in order to know when the farmers work and what they do at different times of the year. There are eight days in the Kejom Ketinguh week and one of them, *kyézhíŋ* '4th weekday' is sacred and considered as the 'country Sunday'. No one is allowed to work in their farm on this day and only community work can be done. It is on this day that people go out to work on roads or to clean up around their houses. There may be meetings in quarters to discuss issues of village development and in the afternoons people meet in njangi[5] houses for financial transactions. The following day, *ə̀zhíŋ* '5th weekday', is usually a day to work on the Fon's farm if it is the season. *Àjùŋ* '3rd weekday' on its part is a 'semi country Sunday' during which farmers are expected to work only half a day. Traditional marriages are conducted on the evenings of *àjùŋ*.

---

[5] This is a system of financial support whereby people come together regularly such as on a monthly basis and contribute money and members take turns to benefit from the contributions. Most farmers use their shares as capital to invest in their farms.

The months of the year are named following agricultural activities or significant events such that *sàŋ ə̀ chù ə̀wú* 'March' literally means the month during which the rainy season starts. It is followed by *sàŋ ə̀ wyé ə̀fó* 'April' or the month of planting while *sàŋ ə̀ pfì àsáŋ* 'July' is the month of harvesting maize. In November grasshoppers always come to the green fields of Kwighe and the month is called *sàŋ ə̀ mbvèn* 'November' meaning month of grasshoppers.

The following table shows the agricultural calendar of some crops cultivated in Kejom Ketinguh as well as the period of land preparation, planting, tendering and harvesting.

Crops cultivated		Dry season			Rainy season								
		Nov	Dec	Jan	Feb	Mar	Apr	May	Jun	Jul	Aug	Sept	Oct
cereals, legumes and grains	*maize												
	**maize												
	*beans												
	**beans												
	*groundnuts												
	**groundnuts												
	*soya beans												
	**soya beans												
roots and tubers	*cocoyams												
	**cocoyams												
	colocasia												
	*potatoes												
	**potatoes												

82

yams												
cassava												
*sweet potatoes												
**sweet potatoes												
vegetables	*tomatoes, leaks, onion, njamanjama											
	**tomatoes, leaks, onion, njamanjama											
perennial crops	coffee											
	plantain/banana											

*First farming period   land preparation ────   Crop tendering ⋯⋯
** Second farming period   Planting ─ ─ ─ ─   Harvesting ═══

Table 9: Agricultural Calendar for some Major Crops in Kejom Ketinguh
Source: Tubah Sub-divisional Delegation of Agriculture and Rural Development and 2014 Field Work

The agricultural calendar shows the planting and harvesting period for the different crop varieties. For all crops, the farming season begins with the search for and preparation of suitable plots. Here, men do the clearing while women do the hoeing. Planting comes thereafter depending on the different crop varieties. Crop tendering is done by weeding and mulching thereby paying more attention to the crops. Three categories of crops are distinguished; seasonal, annual and perennial crops with different agricultural calendars.

Seasonal crops are crops with a brief vegetation cycle from planting through weeding to harvesting. They include maize, beans, soya beans, groundnuts, potatoes, njamanjama and tomatoes. These crops follow seasonal variation such that planting begins in March with the beginning of the rains and harvesting is done after 4 - 6 months. Land preparation starts immediately for dry season cultivation and the process continues all year round for some crops.

The second category is the annual crops with a vegetative cycle that ranges from 6 to 12 months. They include cocoyams, colocasia, yams, sweet potatoes, and cassava. These crops do not follow seasonal variation although most often, planting begins in March and the crop needs at least 6 months to mature before harvesting can be done. A second planting can be done immediately after the harvest but for most of them planting is done only once a year.

The last variety includes the perennial crops such as coffee, raffia palm and bananas whose vegetative cycle exceeds one year. Agricultural activities for these crops are spread almost throughout the year as planting and harvesting take place anytime except coffee that can only be planted between March and April.

In a whole it is important that we observe the general manner in which the soils of Kejom Ketinguh are used. Some areas are shown in figure 5 to be reserved for the rearing of cattle, others for cultivation of crops, others for settlement, etc.

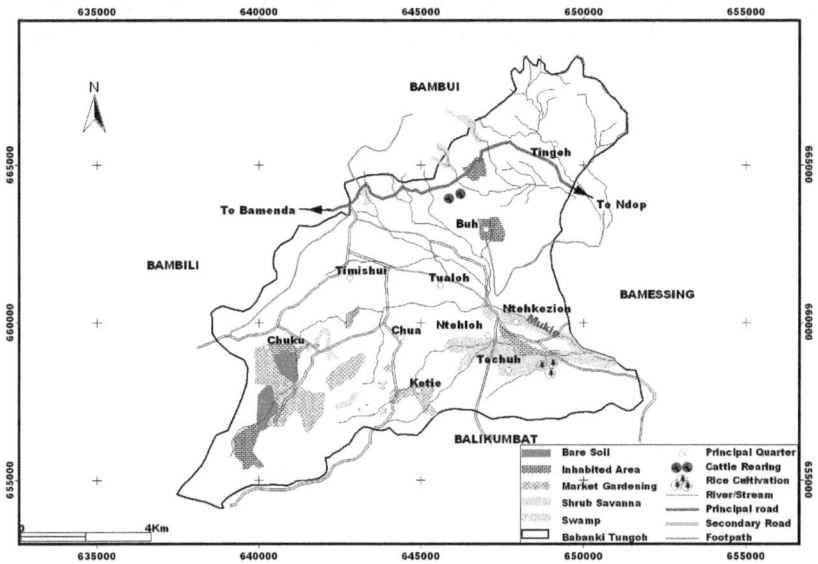

Figure 5: Soil Occupation in Kejom Ketinguh
Source: CAMGIS DBMS (2013)

As far as agriculture is concerned we can note the dominant activities such as market gardening, cattle rearing and rice cultivation in the swamps of Techuh. The road network too is dense although there are mostly secondary roads and footpaths. Some bare soils exist due to the rugged nature of the relief.

6.3 Conclusion

The systems of farming adopted by the people have been surveyed and presented in this chapter. It has also been illustrated that apart from the traditional farming methods of slash and burn or mulch, shifting cultivation and bush fallowing that continue to be practised, the night paddock manuring system has been introduced and this has increasingly promoted agricultural activities in the village. Furthermore, it has been shown that the stages involved in farming such as the periods of planting, weeding and harvesting are based on the rainy and dry seasons of the Kejom Ketinguh area.

CHAPTER SEVEN
PROBLEMS FACED BY FARMERS

7.0 Introduction

Farming in Kejom suffers from a number of setbacks. The problems involved here can be divided into pre-harvest and post-harvest problems.

7.1 Pre-harvest Difficulties

These are problems related to availability of land, its fertility, and availability of capital which are supposed to accompany the farmer towards greater productivity.

7.1.1 Soil Fertility

Farming activities in Kejom are greatly affected by the fertility of the soil. Though the soils are of volcanic origin in Kwighe in particular, they are gradually losing fertility due to seasonal erosion which carries the soils down to the lower plains of Tikebeng and certain practices such as the use of chemical fertilizers that have killed soil organisms. The practice of the ankara system has equally contributed to the soils losing their fertility. Overgrazing on the land has equally accelerated soil erosion, Even though the farmers have resorted to the night paddocking manuring system, soil infertility still remains a problem especially in the cultivation of food crops.

7.1.2 Slope Gradient

Farming here is also affected by the steep slope gradient. Soils along steep slopes are poor and difficult to till for cultivation of crops. Some of the slopes are hardly accessible. Cattle equally suffer from the hands of steep slopes and that is one reason why transhumance sets in during the dry season as the herdsmen take the cattle away from such slopes and go to lowlands that have grass.

7.1.3 Pests and Diseases

Pests and diseases affect plant growth in Kejom Ketinguh. Weeds, parasitic plants and insects hinder plant growth and productivity. They either compete with sown crops for plant nutrient or destroy the crop before it is harvested. Many weeds (especially *àshùŋ* 'elephant grass', and *kɜ̀zɔ̀yn* 'spear grass') render tilling operations difficult. Pests such as weevils and fungi eat up and destroy crops such as maize, beans and njamanjama, leading to a reduction in the output. Insects such as ants, crickets sometimes destroy crops.

7.1.4 Abandonment of Coffee Farms

Amongst reasons advanced for the poor performance of the coffee sector in the village is the increasing abandonment of coffee production by most farmers. Many farmers continue to cut down their coffee plants in favour of food crops that may yield twice or thrice a year and sell faster and better. It is difficult to find a farmer in Kejom Ketinguh who specializes in coffee production. People just have patches of coffee farms that they exploit in an uninteresting manner. There is no maintenance, no application of fertilisers nor spraying against diseases as it was done in the past.

7.1.5 Scare Arable Land

The more reason why farmers are forfeiting coffee farms for food crops is because the farms themselves are increasingly becoming scarce. There is an exponential growth in population which is not commensurate with growth in land. In order to compensate for the shortage, the scare land is used for many purposes. Besides the cultivation of food crops, the land is used for construction of houses to accommodate people and development structures. Even where the farms are available most of them are old and have lost their fertility. Even though there is a lot of solidarity, land ownership techniques have greatly contributed to scarce land. While some people lack land elsewhere in the village some farmers have extensive uncultivated parcels.

7.1.6 Difficult Access to Funds

The farming sector equally suffers from the problem of inadequate capital to buy farm inputs and equipment. Farming is still carried out with rudimentary tools such as machetes and hoes. Farmers acquire their capital from personal savings and borrowing which sometimes creates conflicts between the farmers when yields are not sufficient to cover the cost and provide profit. In the past, coffee farmers depended on cooperatives to get fertilizers and other inputs. Today, these cooperatives no longer exist. The farmers could have turned to specialized banks to revamp production but these banks are not available and other financial institutions do not provide for easy access to credit.

7.1.7 Illiteracy and Conservatism

Farming in Kejom is affected by illiteracy and conservatism. Most farmers are uneducated and sometimes refuse to adopt new techniques of farming. In Kwighe for example, NGOs such as CIPCRE, INADES Formation have imparted farmers with new farming techniques, night paddocking and dairy farming yet many of them are still reluctant to adopt the new methods.

7.1.8 Farmer-grazier Conflicts

In Kwighe in particular where cattle rearing and farming are done next to each other, conflicts between farmers and graziers are common. Cattle often destroy crops in their search for pastures. This does not only affect output but the relationship between cattle rearers and farmers. This is problematic especially as they need to exchange services during night paddocking.

7.2 Post-harvest Problems

These are the problems that the farmers encounter after they have harvested their crops from the farms. What do they do next? Some of these obstacles include:

7.2.1 Transportation Difficulties

This is one of the major problems that affect farmers in this part of Cameroon. It is often said that production is not complete until the product reaches the final consumer. This is the situation in Kejom Ketinguh and especially in Kwighe where the terrain is difficult, with a hilly relief, rough and rugged, making construction of roads difficult. Although there is an intensive cultivation of market gardening crops here, the farm to market roads are limited. Most farms are linked by footpaths developed on the steep slopes. Farm outputs are mostly transported from the farms on head, assisted today by motorbikes on the narrow tracks. The harvesting of crops in this area entails arrangement with motorbikes that will transport these crops to accessible areas. The roads are also seasonal, being very muddy during the rainy season and dusty during the dry season. The only market which is near the tarred road is the Kyephen market from where crops are taken to neighbouring towns. The main road that links the upper and lower parts of Kejom Ketinguh is almost inaccessible during the rainy season. The poor nature of the roads in Kejom Ketinguh has resulted to breakdown of vehicles during the rainy season, leading to spoilage of perishable market gardening products; high transportation costs resulting to high prices of these products in the market; as well as time wastage due to the roundabout movements, as the roads do not follow direct courses.

7.2.2 Commercialization of the Produce

The marketing of what is produced in the farms is equally a serious challenge to Kejom Ketinguh farmers. As far as market gardening crops are concerned, the farmers suffer from the influence of middlemen or the 'bayamsellam'. A bag of njamanjama could be sold at 2,500FCFA during the normal season at the level of the village or 5,000FCFA during the dry season. But in the urban areas of Yaoundé and Douala, the price is above 10,000FCFA. The 'bayamsellam' make more profit than those who cultivate, taking into consideration the heavy task of weeding and harvesting this vegetable. The middlemen just come, hand over bags to the farmers and collect the bags filled with njamanjama at the end of the day. They take it back to Yaoundé and Douala and give out to retailers at exorbitant prices.

7.2.3 Poor Storage Facilities

Most harvested crops such as maize and beans get infested with weevils because of poor storage. Though the farmers try to protect the crops by using wood ash, they sometimes suffer losses before the season runs out. They are sometimes forced to sell crops at give-away prices to avoid loss. Crop damage is particularly acute in case of crops such as cabbages, carrot, and tomatoes amongst others.

7.3 Proposals to Remedy Farming Difficulties in Kejom Ketinguh

It is essential that the problems that are trying to slow down this sector of activity should be addressed. This is so because agriculture is the main activity of the people, so if care is not taken, problems of famine and diverse conflicts will eventually interrupt the stability witnessed in the village today. Implementing any of the following proposals may ensure the continuous productivity of the agricultural sector of Kejom Ketinguh.

7.3.1 Setting up Cooperatives

Farmers in Kejom Ketinguh face a lot of problems in distributing and selling their produce. When the harvest is good and farmers have surpluses they usually lose large quantities. For example, the perishable vegetables such as njamanjama, carrots, tomatoes, etc., cannot be stored for a long period of time, and there is no market news service available to the farmers. There is a long chain of middlemen who merely take away part of the money that would have gone to the farmers. The transportation and storage facilities are not only inadequate but also expensive. Creating cooperative sales' societies can be a way to help the farmers get a fair return of their labour and surpluses.

A cooperative, as used here, refers to the unification of farmers or farms belonging to many small holder farmers. Cooperative sale or marketing is a voluntary association of farm producers for the joint sale of their produce. It can be described as a system whereby groups of farmers voluntarily pool their resources and join together to carry on some or all of the processes in the marketing of agricultural produce.

The farmers of Kejom Ketinguh can therefore join in this venture and even go further to collaborate in procuring credit and inputs for their farming activities. Kejom Ketinguh can operate a number of cooperatives following the diversity of the crops produced. There can be cooperatives specialized in marketing tapioca, onion, tomatoes, njamanjama and maize amongst others. A central storage facility could be set up for each cooperative. The cooperative through their assembling points can arrange for the collection and sale of the different products of the members. They will therefore be charged with storage, transportation and distribution or sales at the best prices for the benefit of the producers.

7.3.2 Adopt the ERI Initiative

ERI refers to Enabling Rural Innovation. The ERI initiative uses participatory research approaches to strengthen the capacity of research and development partners as well a rural communities to access and generate technical and market information for improving farmers' decision making. This initiative has emerged from three main streams of farmer participatory research, rural agro-enterprise development and natural resource management. Using the most effective elements from these three areas, the ERI aims to build more robust livelihood strategies within rural communities.

The ERI approach focuses on building the skills and knowledge of communities, local service providers and farmers' organizations to engage effectively in markets. Once the group has selected the most appropriate option, the farmer organization or group then follows a stepwise approach to develop a sustainable enterprise. The process begins with a participatory diagnosis which assesses community assets, market opportunities and constraints. An enterprise planning committee is elected to undertake market studies on behalf of the group. Participatory market research builds skills of farmers to analyze markets and permits them to have a better understanding, consolidate relationships with traders and to negotiate for better prices for their produce. The involvement of farmers as decision makers in all stages of the innovation process is a hallmark of the ERI approach. Each farmer group is supported by a development facilitator who oversees the development of the group. With increased maturity, groups report dramatic increases in levels of trust and cooperation. The presence of several groups, regular group meetings and regular interaction with research and development partners can lead to linking up of groups which will attract additional resources from government agencies, NGOs and other rural service providers.

Successful innovations result from strong interactions and flow of knowledge within networks of stakeholders. Effective local partnerships between researchers, extension workers, NGOs and farmer communities are the key to the success of ERI. Partners are selected not only for their interest in incorporating the approach into their ongoing work, but also on the basis of institutional assessment, including their working relationships with local communities, their objectives and potential to scale up impact.

An important aspect of farm to market linkages is a crucial aspect of research in order to sustain the increases in productivity. ICTs are particularly instrumental in these linkages.

Kejom Ketinguh as an agricultural landscape can benefit from such a strategy and become a production pole in the Northwest Region in particular and Cameroon in general.

7.3.3 Create an Agricultural Information Centre for Kejom Ketinguh

An information centre comprising of a traditional library, furnished with newsletters, books and other materials on agricultural practice as well as a modern facility including internet services, CD-technology, etc, can assist the population to integrate more ICTs in their activities and increase agricultural productivity. This centre should be a farmer centred information centre where the stakeholders will work together with the farmers to ensure better productivity.

The research centre will ensure the transfer of technology and information on improved species; weather stations will provide the weather data and advice on how to cope with weather situations; and mobile personnel will make contacts with markets to inquire prices of products in the market as well as farm inputs. The centre will provide a network system through the use of modern and traditional ICTs, both in and out of the village. In this way farmers will know what to produce, when to produce and for whom, such that there will be no wastage and quality production will be guaranteed. Figure 6 demonstrates how such a centre can function.

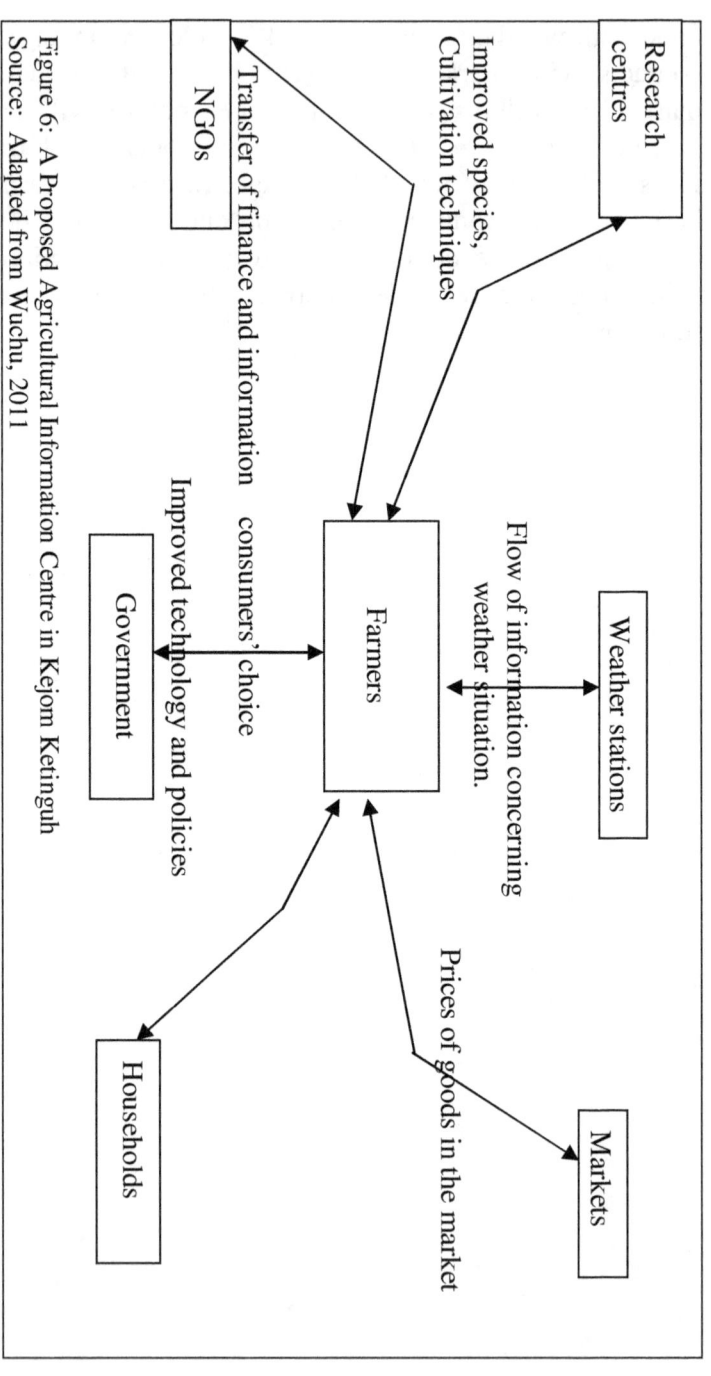

Figure 6: A Proposed Agricultural Information Centre in Kejom Ketinguh
Source: Adapted from Wuchu, 2011

If any of these proposals is implemented it will go a long way to solve problems related to production and marketing. The farmers will be able to plant crops on suitable soils and at the right time and also sell at better prices.

7.4 Conclusion

In this chapter some of the challenges that the farmers face have been shown to include both pre- and post- harvest problems. Natural factors such as soil fertility, slope gradient, pests and diseases, scarce arable land, and human factors such as the abandonment of coffee farms, lack of funding, illiteracy and conservatism and farmer-grazier conflicts constitute some of the pre-harvest problems. After harvesting the farmers usually have difficulties in transporting, commercializing and storage or preservation of their crops. Finally, proposals have been made to remedy the problems and in this regard it has been proposed that the farmers could adopt the Enabling Rural Innovation system and create an agricultural information centre for themselves through which their agricultural activities will be regulated and enhanced.

Not every aspect of agriculture in Kejom Ketinguh has been addressed in this book but we expect that the ideas and information presented here could stimulate reflections and further studies on this sector which represents the essence of the Kejom Ketinguh community.

REFERENCES

Akumbu, P. W. 1999. Nominal Phonological Processes in Babanki. MA dissertation, University of Yaoundé 1.

Akumbu, P. W. 2008. *Kejom (Babanki) – English Lexicon*. Ga'a Kejom Development Committee. Bamenda: AGWECAMS.

Akumbu, P. W. 2009. Kejom Tense System. In Tanda, V., P. Tamanji, & H. Jick. (eds.), *Language, Literature and Social Discourse in Africa: Essays in honour of Emmanuel N. Chia*. Buea: University of Buea. pp. 183-200.

Akumbu, P. W. 2011. Tone in Kejom (Babanki) Associative Construction. *Journal of West African Languages*. Volume 38, No 1: 69-88.

Akumbu, P. W. & E. Fogwe. 2012. *A Pedagogic Grammar of Babanki*. Köln: Rüdiger Köppe Verlag.

Butah, P. 2003. Land Degradation and Conservation in Tubah Sub-Division, DIPESS II dissertation, ENS, University of Yaoundé 1.

Cameroon Geographic Information System, Data Base Management System 2 (CAMGIS DBMS). 2013.

Fellmann, J., A. Getis & J. Getis. 1997. *Human Geography; Landscapes of Human Activities, fifth edition, Madison, London, Brown and Benchmark*.

Franzel, S. & Van Houten, H. 1992. *Research with Farmers. Lessons from Ethiopia*. CAB International.

Helvetas-Cameroon. 2001. Monographic Study of Tubah Rural Council.

Hyman, L. M. 1979. Tonology of the Babanki Noun. *Studies in African Linguistics*. 10:159-178.

Hyman, L. M. 1980. Babanki and the Ring Group. In *L'Expansion Bantoue*. Paris: SELAF. 225-258.

Kaganzi. 2003. Farmer Participation in Market Research to Identify Income Generating Opportunities: CIAT Africa Highlight, Number 9.

Lewis, M. P., F. S. Gary & C. D. Fennig (eds.). 2014. *Ethnologue: Languages of the World*, 17th edition. Dallas,

Texas: SIL International. Online version: http://www.ethnologue.com.
Menang, T. 1981. A Special Language for a Special Speaker. Ms.
Menang, T. 1983. Word Classes in Ga'a Kejom. Ms.
Mutaka, M. N. & E. Phubon. 2006. Vowel Raising in Babanki. *Journal of West African Languages.* Vol. 33, N° 1: 71-88.
Ndenecho, E. N. 2005. Appraisal of NGO Intervention in Natural Resource Management in Tubah Upland Watershed. Paper presented at the Helvetas sponsored Norm Formative Evolution Workshop, 10-17th January 2000. Helvetas, Bamenda.
Ngwega, D. A. 2007. Agricultural Adaptation to Socio-economic Changes among Peasants in Bambui, North West Province, Cameroon, Maîtrise dissertation, University of Yaoundé 1.
Ntangsi, V. 2000. Socio-cultural Aspects of Kejom Ketinguh. Ms
Nwequeh, A. B. 2002. The Strive for Sustainable Agricultural Land Management in Tubah Sub-Division, North West Province Cameroon. Maîtrise dissertation, University of Yaoundé 1.
Phubon, E. 1999. Aspects of Babanki Phonology. Long Essay for the award of a B.A in linguistics. University of Buea.
Phubon, E. 2002. Phonology of the Babanki Verb. Masters' dissertation. University of Buea.
Phubon, E. 2007. Lexical Phonology of Babanki. DEA Dissertation. University of Yaoundé I.
Tamanji, P. N. 1987. Phonology of Babanki. Post Graduate Diploma, University of Yaoundé.
Tubah Council. 2006. Introducing Tubah Council.
Velem, P. Y. 2013. The Influence of Relief on Land Use: The case of Babanki Tungoh-Tubah Sub-Division, DIPESS II Dissertation, University of Bamenda.
Watters, J. 2003. Grassfields Bantu. In Nurse, D. and Philippson, G. (eds.), *The Bantu Languages.* New York: Routledge, 225-256.

Wombong, D. K. 2003. Man's Activities in Soils in Babanki Tungoh, Maîtrise dissertation, University of Yaoundé 1, 130p.

Wuchu, C. W. 2011. ICTs, Agricultural Change and the Development of Tubah Sub-Division. University of Yaoundé 1.

Web References

www.ciat-library.ciat.cgiar,org/articulos_ciat/s7_kaaria-ful.pdf, accessed on July 16, 2014 at 10am.

www.cipcre.org, accessed on August 23, 2014 at 8am

www.kedjomketinguh.org/history, accessed on September 16, 2014 at 10am

www.s-cool.co.uk/gcse/geography/agriculture/revise-it/farming-as-a-system, accessed on September 16, 2014 at 11am.

APPENDICES

1. The Kejom Alphabet

A	a	*àsáŋ*	sweet corn
B	b	*ə̀bí*	kola nut
Bv	bv	*bvù*	grind
Ch	ch	*chì*	in-law
D	d	*dém*	play
Dz	dz	*ndzàm*	axe
E	e	*tén*	push
Ə	ə	*ə̀kə̀'*	face (n)
F	f	*ə̀fwóf*	wind
G	g	*gùf*	be pregnant
Gh	gh	*ə̀ghàm*	mat
I	i	*tyín*	cut
Ɨ	ɨ	*kə̀kɨ*	chair
J	j	*jòm*	dream (n)
'	'	*kə̀vú'*	mushroom
K	k	*kə̀kú*	offering
L	l	*ə̀lò*	bridge
M	m	*mó*	lake
N	n	*ə̀nòn*	herd
Ny	ny	*nyò'*	write
Ŋ	ŋ	*ŋàŋ*	energy
O	o	*bò*	two
Pf	pf	*pfè*	cook (v)
S	s	*sám*	migrate
Sh	sh	*ə̀shɨ*	eye
T	t	*ə̀tó*	hut
Ts	ts	*tsòŋ*	thief
U	u	*ŋgù'*	stone
ʉ	ʉ	*kə̀ghʉ*	foot
V	v	*ə̀ví*	tadpole
W	w	*wùlɨm*	man

Y	y	yén	see
Z	z	kə̀zòŋ	thanks
Zh	zh	ə̀zhú	time
High Tone	v́	tám	plan
Low Tone	v̀	wɩ̀'	person

NB: The transcription used in this lexicon is broadly the one used in the orthography. The orthographic symbols which are different from the International Phonetic Alphabet (IPA) have the following equivalents:

IPA	Transcription
ʃ	sh
tʃ	ch
dʒ	j
ɣ	gh
ʔ	'
ɲ	ny
j	y

2. Days of the Week

No	Day	Orthography
1	kyépfèn	Kyephen
2	wyéŋgáŋ	Wengang
3	àjùŋ	Ajung
4	kyézhíŋ*	Kyezhing
5	ə̀zhíŋ	Zhing
6	ə̀mbítyélə́	Mbityele
7	ə̀mbíwí	Mbiwi
8	ə̀lè	Leh

* kyézhíŋ is the village Sunday, the day people are expected not to do any personal farm work. Anyone found working on their farm on this day would be penalized. People may do

community work such as road maintenance or cultivating the Fon's farm.

3: Months of the Year

No	Month	Phonetic Form	Event	Gloss
1	sàŋ ə̀ lìm	sòə̀ lìm	dry season	January
2	sàŋ ə̀ kə̀ntó lìm	sòə̀ kə̀ntólìm	peak of dry season	February
3	sàŋ ə̀ chừ ə̀wú	sòə̀ chừwừ	start of rainy season	March
4	sàŋ ə̀ wyé ə̀fó	sòə̀ wyéfó	planting	April
5	sàŋ ə̀ sì àbúʔ	sòə̀ sì àbùʔ	harvesting pumpkin	May
6	sàŋ ə̀ zàʔsə̀ kə̀fừʔ	sòə̀ záʔsə̀ kə̀fừʔ	second weeding	June
7	sàŋ ə̀ pfì àsáŋ	sòə̀ pfì àsáŋ	harvesting maize	July
8	sàŋ ə̀ àsáŋ ə́ ŋgwú	sòə̀ àsó ŋgwú	planting dry season maize	August
9	sàŋ ə̀ fə̀nsàʔ	sòə̀ fə̀nsàʔ	frog's month	September
10	sàŋ ə̀ fə̀nshìʔ	sòə̀ fə̀nshìʔ	grass beetles' month	October
11	sàŋ ə̀ mbvèn	sòə̀ mbvèn	grasshoppers' month	November
12	sàŋ ə̀ shwáyn	sòə̀ shwàyn	transition from rainy to dry season	December

4. Some Crops Grown in Kejom Ketinguh

Crop	Scientific Name	Gloss
àsáŋ	Zea mays	maize
kàsá	Manihot esculenta	cassava
ə̀làŋ ə́káʔə́ káʔə́	Colocasia esculenta	colocasia (Taro)
àkwén	Phaseolus vicia	beans
àlém	Dioscorea alata	yams
ə̀làŋ ə́ mə̀ŋkáʔə̀	Xanthosoma sagittifolium	cocoyams
kòfí	coffea Arabica	arabica coffee
bə́lə̀ŋ	Arachis hypogaea	groundnut

àbú?	Cucurbita pepo	pumpkins
ndɔ̀ŋ ə̀ mə̀ŋká?ə̀	Solanum tuborsum	potato
ndɔ̀ŋ ə́ lyɨ̀má	Ipomeo batatas	sweet potato
àlyù?	Raphia africana	raffia palms
àkwén ə́ mə̀ŋká?ə̀	Oryza sativa	paddy rice
mbàsə̀ ə́ pfɨ́?ə́	Solanum scrabum	njamanjama
fə̀nyɔ́? fə́ mə̀ŋká?ə̀	Solanum lycopersicum	tomato
fə̀nyɔ́?	Solanum melongena	garden egg
fə̀sés	Solanaceae capsicum	pepper
byə́	Persea americana	avocado
mə́ŋgwòlə̀	Mangifera indica	mango
kə̀nsáŋsáŋ	Ananas comosus	pineapple
kə̀nsáŋsáŋ	Saccharum	sugarcane
ə̀ŋgɔ̀m	Musa acuminata/balbisiana	bananas/plantains
ə̀byɨ	Vitellaria paradoxa	shea butter nut
ŋgwŏbàŋ	Psidium guajava	guava
lâmsə̀	Citrus sinensis	orange
kə̀mbáynmbáyn kə́ ntàŋ	Passiflora edulis	Passion fruit
dzàŋ	Gypohierax angolensis	palm nut
kə̀nwì?tə̀	Fragaria ananassa	strawberry
tə̀wás	Pisum sativum	cow peas
kə̀zhɨ́ŋ	Vernonia amygdalina	bitter leaf
nshínsə́	Pisum sativum	dried cow peas
ŋgɔ̀lɔ̀?	Abelmoschus esculentus	okra
sòyà bīns	Glycine max	soya beans
kábéj	Brassica oleracea	cabbage
gálìk	Allium sativum	garlic
ányɔ̀s	Allium cepa	onion
káròt	Daucus carota	carrot
líks	Allium ampeloprasum	leeks
grín bīns	Phaseolus vulgaris	green beans
kə̀ntsù?	aframomum melegueta	unknown
kə̀sàkàlyù?	annona senegalensis	unknown

dzè	vitex doniana	unknown
kə̀mbáynmbáyn	vitex madiensis	unknown

5. Some Farming Terminology

Word or Phrase	Gloss	Word or Phrase	Gloss
ə́shyɛ̀ʔ ə̀sɨ́m	work a farm	kə̀nsé	sharpener
kə̀bwin	ridge	chúŋ	dig
kə̀nchɔ́m	cutting down grass	kɔ́m	finalize
ə̀sɨ́m	farm	chɨ̀	place affliction
ə̀kú	forest (for farming)	chɨ́sə́	affliction
byɨ̀ kə̀bwìn	furrow	báʔlə́	sell
nyɨ̀	machete	zén	buy
shɨ̀	hoe	nzén	buyer
ə̀káŋ	barn	chɔ́ʔ	borrow/lend
ŋgwàʔ	seed	tsɔ́ŋ	steal
súʔə́ ə̀sɨ́m	weed	ŋkɨ́m	basket
zàʔsə̀ kə̀fù̀ʔ	second weeding	kə̀kyè	basket
wyé	plant	ə̀wɔ́ŋ	market
mɔ̀ʔ	plant (by spreading)	nyùʔ	burn
pfɨ̀ àsáŋ	harvest maize	sénsə́/tɔ́ŋtə́	invite people to assist
káŋ ɔ́ mbàsə̀	harvest njamanjama	táʔ	entertain
kwɔ̀ŋ	harvest (fruit)	tɔ́mə́	protect (farm)
chə́ (ndɔ̀ŋ)	work (sweet potato)	tsɨ̀ŋ	guard (farm)

6. Kejom Ketinguh Quarters

Ntehloh	Chibam
Mbansanjih	Chuku
Kenkung	Chua
Nkasah	Timenshui
Tekhuh	Ketieh
Mbohboh	Alumbyeh
Techuh	Badem

Tsohmbe	Bambekwen
Tiku	Mbuafon
Chukebang	Chufyeh
Mphewen	Chuketam
Makwendzam	Nsem
Ntehkezoin	Kechukekebih
Nguhbyi	Chualuh
Ntehmbih Fetang	Nsohnsoh
Buh Fedzam	Tibam
Buh Fengam	Tsih
Mbuaten Kensansang	Chiashung
Mbuaten Tengom	Mbuaveshom
Tualoh	Febum
Fendieng	Feshinzhing
Tingeh	Tishung
Fengyeh	Tohkedzam

7. Some Kejom Folklore
A) mə̀tǐtì 'Folktales'

1) **Tɔ̀lɔ́kjí nə̀ fə̀tʃwí**
Narrator: ntìə̀
Audience: mbòó
Narrator: tɔ̀lɔ́kjí nlŭ ló
Audience: ò
Narrator: mə́kjíʔə́ tɔ́f nɔ́ʔə̀ nàntô. ə̀ ə̀tʃúʔə́ lájn yə̀ dʒù̀ kwètə́ fə̀tʃwí ə̀ mə̀ gàʔ à fə̀tʃwí fə́ lá jì zì jì ɲíŋə̀ tʃòə̀ wɛ́n. fə̀tʃwí fə́ ŋkjí lí wɛ́n tjínə̀ wɛ́n fwí. yə̀ bə́m lá wù kə̀ʔə̀ kó ndíʔ á wù zì wù né nɔ́ʔə̀ kə̀ɲù̀ kə̀tsɛ́n ŋgáʔá wù zì wù ɲíŋə̀ tʃò mò ló. tà àndə́ tɔ̀lɔ́kjí ŋkjíʔə́ tɔ́f nɔ́ʔə̀ nàntô lì yə̀ə́ mbjímə́ lí áwɛ́n lá jì zì jì ɲíŋə̀ tʃòə̀ wɛ́n. ɔ́kéì tjínə̀ fə̀tʃwí fə́ mfwí lí yə̀ gáʔə́ və́ wú tà kə̀tsí kə́ kə́ɲíŋ á kjìkə́. fə̀tʃwí fə́ mə́ gàʔə̀ kíə́ bjɛ̀ʔə̀ yə̀ kíə́ kə̀wú kə́ kə́ɲíŋ nɔ́ʔə̀ ŋkàjn.

nɔʔə ə tɔ̀lɔ̀kjí àndə́ ɣə́ ŋkjíʔə́ tɔ́f lì ɣə̀ə́ ndʒʉ́ lúwèn mpfʉ́tə́ və̀ləmə vɔ́ wén. múʔə́ wénə fə̀tʃwí fə́ mə́ jì gà? ŋwʉ́ kə̀ʃí á vɔ́ né ndʒʉ́ bùmtə̀ tsú. lá vɔ́ á nlù kə̀ɲíŋ fá ʃə̀ vɔ́ tìmə́ á kə̀ʃí kə́ kəkjè. nè lù fá ʃə̀ vɔ́ tìmə́ á kə̀ʃí kə́ kəkjè. ɣə̀ə́ tɔ̀lɔ̀kjí ndʒʉ́ lúwèn àndə́ ɣə́ jí kjíʔə́ tɔ́f nɔ́ʔə nàntô lì mpfʉ́tə́ vələmə vɔ́ wén mə́ gá? lá kəkjéə́ né tímə́ á ʃə̀, kəkjé tímə́ á fà, kəkjé tímə́ á kə̀ʃí kə́tsén kjì. ŋwʉ́ ə́ dʒʉ́ tá lì nzáʔə́ á kə̀ʃí á kə̀ɲíŋ né dʒʉ́ mè tsú.

ə̀tʃʉ́ʔə́ lájn və̀wénə́ mə́ nzí kə̀ɲʉ́ kə́ kə̀ɲíŋ kjì. nɔ́ʔə ə̀ʒʉ̀ ə kɔ̀ á vɔ́ zí á mə́ɲíŋ, bjè̀ʔə́ fə̀tʃwí fə́ nə́ nzísə́ ŋíŋə́ fə́ ə̀ bjì̀ʔtə́ áʃí ə́ wén ɣə̀ə́ mə́ sə́ ɲíŋə́ dʒʉ̀. bèt á lì mə́ díʔə́ ɲíŋ nɔ́ʔə́ ŋkàjn. àndə́ ɣə́ bjíʔtə́ áʃí ə́ wén mə́, vɔ́ mə́, àndə́ vɔ́ gáʔá, mə́ nzítə́. ɣə̀ə́ sə́ lʉ̀ á kə̀ɲíŋ tɔ̀lɔ̀kjí ntímə́ mə́ ntʃə́?. ŋgáʔá kə̀ŋgʉ̌ kə́ kə́fó, ɣə̀ə́ kó kjíʔə́ tɔ́f. né sə́ dʒʉ́ fʉ̀ á kə̀ʃí, á mbì kə̀ʃi múʔə́ ləmə ə̀ tɔ̀lɔ̀kjí jì sə̀ díʔ tsú. fə̀tʃwí fə́ ŋgáʔá 'á áʔá wʉ̀ sə̀ díʔ á ʃə̀ à mbì mà bó bú lɔ́?' kə̀ɲʉ̀ kjíkə́ ntʃó wén ɣə̀ə́ mbɛ́ mbjíʔtə́ áʃí wén jí mbɛ́ nzítə́ sə́ tʃɔ̀ə́ ndʒʉ̀ tɔ̀lɔ̀kjí tsén jì mbɛ́ ntʃə́? mbwínə́ sə́ ví wén. ɣə̀ə́ mbɛ́ nljí kə̀ɲíŋ nljí kə̀ɲíŋ mbɛ́ sə́ záʔə́ á nùmbà ə̀tá? mbɛ́ njénə́ wén. ɣə̀ə́ ŋgáʔá jì kó ŋkí lá à bè bè dì? jí lɔ́. ɣə̀ə́ mbɛ́ ŋkwʉ́ʔsə́ áwʉ́ ə́ kə̀ɲíŋə́ wén. mbɛ́ sə́ dʒʉ̀ á nùmbà ə̀kà? ɣə̀ bɛ́ díʔ. tá lì fə̀tʃwí fə́ né ɔ́vá ɲíŋ tà àndə́ fə́ ɲíŋə̀ lí nɔ́ʔə nàntô lì mə́ mbwáʔə́ mpfʉ́.

ŋgàjnə́ mə́ mmɛ́ á kə̀ʃí á jèn. tɔ̀lɔ̀kjí mbwínə́ nví sə́ tʃə́ʔə́ wén.

Tortoise and Deer
One day Tortoise who was very wise got up and went to meet Deer. He told Deer that he could run faster than Deer. Deer was so annoyed and asked Tortoise how he could run whereas he is so slow. Tortoise challenged him to a contest. With all the confidence that Deer had in his running skill he told Tortoise to just set a day for the competition. They therefore agreed on a date.

As wise as Tortoise was he went around and pleaded with his brothers to help him win the race especially because they all look alike and cannot be differentiated from one another. He placed them at different stop points along the running tract up to the finish line.

On the day of the competition, they met at the starting point and began. As soon as they took off Deer closed his eyes and began to speed off as fast as he could. As soon as Deer closed his eyes the way he always does when running, Tortoise just stood there and was laughing at him for being so stupid and finally disappeared into the bush. Deer ran to the first stop but to his greatest surprise he met Tortoise who had been standing there. Deer knew that he was the same Tortoise he started off with and so he wondered how possible it was that Tortoise had run faster than him. When Deer took off he again closed his eyes and increased his speed while Tortoise laughed and went his way. Surprisingly again Deer met Tortoise at the next stop a thing which stunned him seriously. At every stop Deer met Tortoise and when he passed he increased his speed but finally he ran himself to death and Tortoise returned and laughed.

This is the end of the story.

2) Màbíʔ á mɔ́ tsɔ́ŋɔ́ àsáŋ ɔ́ wìʔ
Narrator: ntìɔ̀
Audience: mbòó
Narrator: wù ŋgwừʔ nə̀ nlŭ ló
Audience: ò
Narrator: ə̀ kúʔə̀ ʃèʔə̀ ə̀símɔ́ wɛ́n á ɔ́kù ló
Audience: ə̀ŋ
Narrator: ɔ́ né mpfí ásáŋɔ́ wɛ́n ŋwú á ɔ́kù màbíʔɔ́ né sɔ́ ví lúwɛ́n mɔ́ ljìɔ̀ ásáŋɔ́ wɛ́n jí vɔ́ vɔ̀wénɔ́ bvừɔ́ ə̀ lám ə̀ ʒí. ɣɔ̀ɔ́ nè sɔ́ kúʔ á ə̀sím nɔ́ʔə̀ ə̀ʒừ ə̀ kɔ ɣə̀ jèn tà múʔɔ́ vɔ́ jí ʃwàn àsáŋ

mbáʔtə̄ mbvʉ́. ɣə̀ jɛ̀n tà àndə́ və́ jì lám ə̀ sə́ ʒɨ́ə́. kə́ tʃó wén lá kə̀n kə̀ɲʉ̀ kə́ díʔ lá à nèə̀ ɣɔ̀ lɔ́. ɔ́kéì ə̀tʃʉ́ʔə́ nlán kə̀tsí kə̀tsén ɣə̀ə́ mə́ ŋgáʔá jì á jɛ́n nɔ́ʔə̀ kə̀nàʔ kə̀ kə̀ɲʉ̀ kə̀nkə́. ə́ nlú lúwèn ŋkúʔə́ ndʒʉ́ njɛ́n dʒí á və̀wɛ́nə́ vì ŋwʉ́ʔ fá tsú. kə̀ʃí kə́tsɛ́nkə́ díʔ múʔə́ kə́ bísə́ lí nɔ́ʔə̀ ŋkàjn tà wɛ́nə́ tʃìə̀ ŋgə̀ŋ ájì. ɣə̀ə́ múʔə́ jì á jɛ́n nɔ́ʔə̀ kə̀ɲʉ̀ kə̀nkə́. ɣə̀ə́ ŋwjé ə̀ʒíʔ á ə̀tʃɨ nɔ́ʔə̀ ŋkàjn. ŋkɔ̀ʔə́ mbí ŋkjékə́ ɣə̀ə́ nljɨ́ ə́kjékjé vjí ŋwjé á kə̀bàs kə́ kə́ɣén. ŋkúʔə́ ŋwʉ́ʔmə́ á ə̀kàŋ nʒɔ́mtə́ tə́ljə́ŋ tə́ ə̀kàŋ mə́ ŋwʉ́ʔmə́ tsú. ɔ́kéì nè sə́ tsɛ̀n fə̀bɨ́ʔ fjìfə́, mbì wìʔə́ nví mbɨ́ʔə́ ə̀bə́mə́ wén nɔ́ʔə̀ mwìmwin və̀tsɛ́və́ mbúm, və́ ntsɛ́ntə́. və̀wɛ́nə́ ŋkwɛ́n lúwèn mbɛ́ ŋwʉ́ʔmə́. tà àndə́ və́ kwɛ́nə̀ fɔ̀jn jì ɣə̀ə́ nʃíʔə́ ŋwʉ́ʔə́ á kə̀ʃí á ɣə̀ nə́ ŋwʉ́ʔ tsú. ɔ́kéì və̀wɛ́nə́ ŋkwɛ́n lúwèn ŋwʉ́ʔə́. ɣə̀ə́ nʃíʔsə́, ɣə̀ə́ nljɨ́ kə̀kjékjé kə́ ə́ʒìʔ, kə̀tʃʉ́ kə́ fɔ́jn ákjì ndìʔ múʔə́ kə́ kúʔ lí nɔ́ʔə̀ mwìmwin, ŋwʉ́ á, nʃíʔsə́ mmɔ́ʔ á wɛ́nə́ kə̀tʃʉ́ tà ndzìndzì. ɣə́ sə́ fwɨ́ə́ ʃíʔə́ və̀wɛ́nə́ kó jɛ́nə́ fwɨ́ə́ ʃíʔə́ və̀wɛ́nə́ kó jɛ́nə́ sə́tsɛ̀n mbì wìʔə́ njɛ́n mə́ ŋgáʔ
 à báŋ ɣɔ́ á kə̀tʃʉ́ ə̀ kə̀tòtʃʉ́s
 à báŋ ɣɔ́ á kə̀tʃʉ́
 tʃwí í ɨ̄ʔ
ə́ nlú mfʉ́ə̀. wútsɛ́n mbɛ́ sə́ ŋwʉ́ʔ sə́tsɛ̀n ɣə̀ə́ mbɛ́ sə́ kjíʔə́ mbɛ́ njɛ́n. mbɛ́ nʒɨ́mtə́
 à báŋ ɣɔ́ á kə̀tʃʉ́ ə̀ kə̀tòtʃʉ́s
 à báŋ ɣɔ́ á kə̀tʃʉ́
 tʃwí í ɨ̄ʔ
mbɛ́ mfʉ́ə̀. ɛ́ʔ ɛ́é. sə́tsɛ̀n víʔə́ mə́ nzì sə́ kjíʔə́. nɔ́ʔə̀ ndə̀ə́ lì lù ɣə̀ ʒɨ̀mtə́ tá lì ɣə̀ fʉ̀ə̀. mpfɛ́nə̀ kə̀tòtʃʉ́s kjíkə́ à mə́ díʔ fɔ̀jnə̀ və̀wɛ́nə́ jì ɣə̀ə́ kó kɨ́ə́ kə̀ɲʉ̀ á və̀wɛ́nə́ gàʔə̀. ŋgáʔ tá lì ŋgáʔ tá lì. sə́tsɛ̀n ə̀ ə̀ bàʔə́ jí njɛ́n lá və̀wɛ́nə́ sə́ fʉ̀ə̀ ɣɔ́ʔə́ ɣə̀ə́ ntsɛ́ntə́ ə̀ʒíʔ jí nʃʉ́ʔ á wɛ́nə́ kə̀tʃʉ́ nɔ́ʔə̀ ə̀tsɛ̀m. ə̀ və̀wɛ́nə́ mfʉ̀ə̀ ɲɨŋkə́ lúwèn fɔ̀jnə̀ və̀wɛ́nə́ jì mpfɨ ə́ mfwɨ́ə́ mə́ mpfɨ.

àsáŋə́ bàʔə́ jí mbwóŋ lúwèn ɣə̀ə́ kó bè kə́ŋə́ kə̀fó kə́wén nə̀ nlù.

ŋgàjnə́ mə́ mmé á kə̀ʃí á jɛ̀n. pfə̀pfə̀pfə̀, bwí wàjnə̀ wù ɣə̀ə́ ŋkúʔə́ tá bwàbwà? ŋkà wù kúʔə́ tá bwàbwà?.

The Monkeys who stole from the Farmer

Once upon a time a man owned a farm in the forest area. He planted and eventually harvested much corn which he kept in his farm house. Each time he went there he would find that someone had ground his corn, cooked it and ate. He wondered who was stealing from him until one day he decided to find out. He could see the spots the thieves usually sit on and so he made a very big fire and carried some coal, went up into the barn and sat there to wait and see. He also made space between the bamboos in the barn through which he could pass the coal. Soon after, a monkey came and played its stomach like a drum and other monkeys assembled. They went into the house as usual took their sitting positions and their chief sat on its special spot. Because the chief's hair was over grown the man lowered some of the coal into the hair without them noticing. It began to burn down to its head gradually until one of them saw it and sang:
    What is red on chief's head?
    what is so red?
Then he stepped out. The next person soon saw the coal
burning down the chief's hair and also sang:
    What is red on chief's head?
    what is so red?
Then he left too. When each of them would discover it they will sing the same and leave but the chief himself couldn't see it and didn't notice what was going on. When the man noticed that most of them had left he poured the rest of the coal on the chief's head and it burnt him to death. From the day they never stole his corn again.
    This is the end of the story.

3) Tsɔ̀ŋ ə̀ kàsá
Narrator: ntìə̀
Audience: mbòó
Narrator: wù ŋgwʉ̀ʔ nə̀ nlŭ ló
Audience: ò
Narrator: ə̀ ʃẽʔə̀ ə̀símə̀ kàsá ə́ wέn. ə̀símə̀ kàsá ə́ wέn jí bɔ́ sə́ díʔ ə̀tʃʉ́ʔə́ lə̀ làjn á ŋgwʉ̀ʔə́ tsέn dʒìŋ kú . tà àndə́ dʒìŋ kúə̀ lì lùwàjnə́ tsέn mə̀ lù lúwὲn ŋkwòʔ nɔ́ʔə̀ kə̀fó á ɣə̀á ʒɨ́ ɣə̀ə́ kó kɨ́. mə̀ dʒʉ̀ lúwὲn ə̀ dʒʉ̀ ə̀ jὲnə́ ə̀símə́ kàsá jí. tà àndə́ ɣə́ jένə̀ lì mə̀ tʃùŋ kàsá fá tsú. sə́ tʃúŋ kàsá jì múʔə́ wìʔ jí tʃɨ́ʔə̀ lɨ́ ə̀símə́ kàsá ə́ wέn. nɔ́ʔə̀ ə̀ʒʉ̀ ə̀ kɔ̀ ɣə̀ə́ ntʃúŋ kàsá jì nvíə̀ mpfé, mpfé á ntɔ̀jn ɣə̀ə́ mbí. ɣə̀ə́ nὲ sə́ bɔ̀ʔtə̀ lá jì ljé lá ɣə̀ə́ kwʉ́ʔə̀ lɨ́ á mə́ʒɨ́ lɔ́. ntɔ̀jnə́ ntsɔ́ʔə́ mfʉ́ fá tʃɨ́ sə́ ɲíŋə́ dʒʉ̀ ɲíŋə́ dʒʉ̀. lùwàjn dʒʉ̀ə̀ fá wέnə́ bàm. ɲíŋə́ dʒʉ̀ lùwàjn ɲíŋə́ fá wέnə́ bàm. ɣə̀ə́ ɲíŋə́ dʒʉ́ tà àndə́ ɲíŋə́ dʒʉ̀ lì ndʒʉ́ ŋkwέn tá ə́sím jì mbέ mfʉ́ fá ntɔ̀jn jí ŋkwέn á ə́sím jí mbέ mbwínsə́ ntítə́ á kàsà.

tà àndə́ ɣə́ títə̀ lì lùwàjn jí mbέ njlɨ́ ntɔ̀jnə̀ wέn mbwínə́ nvì. mbέ ndʒʉ́ mbέ ndʒʉ́ ntʃúŋ kàsá jì á nùmba☐ àɣájn àbò. àndə́ ɣə́ ntʃúŋə̀ lì nví mpfé kàsá jí né sə́ fʉ̀ʔə̀ fá tʃɨ́ fʉ̀ʔə̀ fʉ̀ʔə̀ fʉ̀ʔə̀ ɣə̀ə́ mbέ sə́ bɔ̀ʔtə̀ lá jì ljé lá ɣə̀ə́ kwʉ́ʔə̀ lɨ́ á mə́ʒɨ́ lɔ́. ntɔ̀jnə́ jí mbέ mfʉ́ tá lì mbέ sə́ ɲíŋə́ dʒʉ̀ ɲíŋə́ dʒʉ̀ ɣə̀ bέ ɲíŋə́ fá wέnə́ bàm. ɣə̀ə́ mbέ ɲíŋə́ ndʒʉ́ dʒʉ́ ŋkwέn tá ə́sím jì mbέ mfʉ́ fá ntɔ̀jn jí mbέ mbwínsə́ ntítə́ á ə̀títɨ́ á tʃì ə̀sìm.

lùwàjn jí njlɨ́ ntɔ̀jnə̀ wέn lúwὲn nvì ŋkwέn á ŋgə̀ŋ ŋkwɔ́ʔtə́ nɔ́ʔə̀ kə̀ɲʉ̀ á ɣə̀á nὲ dʒìŋ mə́ díʔ á wέn ə́wὲn ɣə̀ə́ kó kɨ́ə́. ɣə̀ə́ ŋkwɔ́ʔtə́ ŋkwɔ́ʔtə́ sə́tsὲn ɣə̀ə́ nljɨ́ ʃɨ́ ntʃúŋtə́ mə̀ŋkwòŋkwòŋ tsú ntʃúŋtə́ ntʃúŋtə́ ntʃúŋtə́ ntʃúŋtə́ ntʃúŋtə́ ndʒʉ̀ə́ ŋkwέn á ə̀símə́ kàsá jì. tà àndə́ ɣə́ ntʃúŋtə́ ndʒʉ́ ŋkwέn lì ə́ mə́ ntʃúŋ kàsá mbwínə́ nví nə̀ wέn á ŋgə̀ŋ nví mpfé. nví mpfé nɔ́ʔə̀ ə̀ʒʉ̀ ə̀ kɔ̀ ɣə̀ə́ mbí mbí mbí. ɣə̀ə́ mbέ sə́ bɔ̀ʔtə̀ ljé lá ɣə̀ə́ kwʉ́ʔə̀ lɨ́ á mə́ʒɨ́ lɔ́ ntɔ̀jn jí mbɛ́ ntsɔ́ʔə́ nʃíʔə́ fá tʃí mbɛ́ sə́ ɲíŋə́ dʒʉ̀ lùwàjn jí mə́ kɨ́ lá ɣə́á ntsɔ́ʔə́ á fə̀ŋkwòŋ jì dʒɪ̀ə́ kó á ndíʔə́ ɣə̀ fʉ́ jì ɣáʔ tsú bwɪ̀nə́ vì ʒɨ́. ɣə́ə́ né sə́ ntsɔ̀ʔ lùwàjn jí sə́ dʒʉ̀ə́ záʔə́ mǘʔə́ ɣə̀ə́ bɛ́ tímə́ mfʉ́. ɣə́ə́ tsɔ̀ʔə́ tá lì dʒʉ̀ə́ tà dʒʉ́ə́. tsɔ̀ʔə́ lúə́ dʒʉ̀ə́ tà dʒʉ́ə́. tsɔ̀ʔə́ dʒʉ̀ə́ tà dʒʉ́ə́. ɣə̀ə́ tsɔ́ʔə́ ndʒʉ́ ndʒʉ́ə́ mbɛ́ mbwínə́ ndʒʉ́ ŋkwɛ́n á ə́sɨ́m jí mbɛ́ mbwínə́ mfʉ́ fá ntɔ̀jn mbɛ́ mbwínsə́ ntítə́ á kàsà á tʃì ə̀sɨ̀m.

lùwàjn jí mbɛ́ mbwínsə́ ŋgáʔá jí kó jì tʃûŋtə́ mə̀ŋkwòŋkwòŋ mjì á ŋkàjn mbɛ́ mbwínsə́ nʃítə́ ntʃúŋtə́ ntʃúŋtə́ ntʃúŋtə́ ntʃúŋtə́ mbɛ́ ndʒʉ̀ə́ mbɛ́ ndʒʉ̀ə́ mbɛ́ ndʒʉ̀ə́ ntʃúŋ kàsá jí mbɛ́ nví mpféə́. kàsá jí mbɛ́ né sə́ mbí vì ɣə̀ə́ mbɛ́ bɔ̀ʔtə̀ lá jì ljɛ́ lá ɣə̀ə́ bí lí lɔ́ kàsá jí ntɔ̀jn jí mbɛ́ ntsɔ́ʔə́ fá tʃí sə́ tsɔ́ʔə́ á ŋkwòŋ ɣə̀ə́ bɛ̀ tʃò tà tʃóə́. ə̀ tsɔ̀ʔ ɣə̀ə́ bɛ̀ tʃò tà tʃóə́. ə̀ tsɔ̀ʔ ɣə̀ə́ bɛ̀ tʃò tà tʃóə́. mbɛ́ ndʒʉ́ ŋkwɛ́n tá lì á ə́sɨ́m mbɛ́ mbwínsə́ nlù ntítə́ á ə̀títɨ́.

lùwàjn jí lùwàjn jí nné tá lì. nné tá lì. nné tá lì. ə̀ʒʉ́ ŋkwʉ́ʔ lùwàjn jí mfə́ŋ ə́ mpfʉ́ mǘʔə́ dʒíŋə́ ʒwí lí ə̀wɛ́n. dʒɪ̀ə́ kó díʔə́ ɣə̀ ʒɨ́ kàsá jì tà ndə́ wìʔə́ ə̀sɨ́m ə́ kàsá jì ɣə̀ə́ jí nɛ̀ kə̀fʉ̀ á wɛ́nə́ kàsá. lùwàjn jí sə́ pfɛ̀ə́ ɣə̀ə́ bɛ̀ bwɪ̀nə́ fʉ̀ ɲìŋ tà ŋíŋə́. lùwàjn jí nné tá lì ŋkáʔə́ mfə́ŋ ə́ mpfʉ́.

tá lì ŋgàjn mə̀ bɛ̀ mɛ̀. pfə̀pfə̀pfə̀, ɣə̀ə́ ŋkúʔə́ tá bwàʔ ŋkà wù bɛ́ kúʔə́ tá bwàʔ.

The Cassava Thief
Once upon a woman planted a cassava farm and as it was getting ready famine attacked the village. One woman who didn't have what to eat decided to go and steal some of the cassava. It happened that the cassava owner had placed medicine against theft on the farm. The woman dug up the cassava, went home and cooked it. When it was ready she opened the pot to dish it out and eat but as soon as she took off the lid, the pot jumped off the fireplace and began to run to the

farm while the woman followed to try to catch it. When the pot got to the farm all the cassava left and went back to the plant in the ground. The woman tried again the second time and exactly the same thing happened. She took her pot home and contemplated on what to do with all the hunger in her. Finally she decided to use her hoe and make little holes on the road so that they will act as obstacles to the pot and she will be able to catch it when it attempts to run again. She then went back and dug the cassava. When it was ready she open the pot to dish it and the pot left again and began to run away. It will fall into a hole but before the woman gets there it would jump out and this continued until they got back to the farm. The cassava left the pot and went back to its plant in the ground. The woman went back and improved on the depth of the holes thinking that she hadn't dug them well the first time. Unfortunately for her the same thing happened the next time she tried. This went on until the woman died of hunger because the owner had kept medicine against theft in her cassava farm.

This is the end of the story.

4) Wàjn ə̀tó kə̀tʃú nə̀ mə̀bú?
Narrator: ntìə́
Audience: mbòó
Narrator: wù ŋgwʉ̀ʔ nə̀ nlǔ ló
Audience: ò
Narrator: ə̀ bwì wàjnə́ wɛ́n ló.
Audience: ò
Narrator: ə̀tʃʉ́ʔ ə́ nlájn ɣə̀ə́ mə́ sə́ dʒʉ́ə́ ʃə́tə́ áljú?ə́ wɛ́n ɣə̀ə́ nè vì tɔ́m ɣə̀ ljí ndzáŋ ɣə̀ bíʔ.

      ndéléndélé mō wâ
      kùm àfwín fə́ tàs
      jɛ̀ lə̀ lù fá ŋgwʉ̀ʔ
      kùm àfwín fə́ ʒʉ̀ʔ
      ndélé mō wâ
      ndéléndélé mō wâ

àndɔ́ yɔ̀ á bí? lì mɔ̀bí?ɔ́ fʉ̀ fá ɔ́kù ɔ̀ fʉ̀ fʉ̀ fʉ̀ ɔ̀ tsɛ̀ntɔ̀ á wénɔ́ fɔ́tín yɔ̀ɔ́ sɔ́ bí?ɔ́ vɔ́ mɔ́ bénɔ́ bí?ɔ́ vɔ́ mɔ́ bénɔ́. nɛ̀ bénɔ́ bénɔ́ bén ɔ̀ bwá? vɔ́ mɔ̀ kwɛ̀n á ŋgɔ́ŋ lúwɛ̀n, vɔ́ ɔ̀ ɲʉ̀ mɔ́nljú? mjìmɔ́ ɔ̀ ɲʉ̀ ɔ̀ ɲʉ̀ ɔ̀ ɲʉ̀ vɔ̀wenɔ́ mɔ̀ fʉ̀ gɔ̀sɔ̀.
     nɔ́?ɔ́ zɛ́ yɔ̀ né tá lì. wàjnɔ́ wén jìɔ́ mɔ́ né njén tà àndɔ́ yɔ̀ né kɔ́ bɔ̀ŋɔ́ á wén nɔ́?ɔ́ ŋkàjn. ɔ̀tʃʉ́? ɔ́ nlájn kɔ̀tsí kɔ́tsén tì?ɔ́ wénɔ́ sɔ́ nlù yɔ̀ɔ́ mɔ́ ŋgá?á 'bìbá màɔ́ né á ʒʉ́sɔ́ ɔ̀ bí?ɔ́ ndzáŋ ɔ̀ mɔ̀kúmɔ́ bén.' yɔ̀ɔ́ ŋgá?á 'kɔ́ né mwɔ̀m', mɔ̀bí?ɔ́ bén. yɔ̀ɔ́ ŋgá?á 'kɔ́ né mwɔ̀m bjɛ̀?ɔ́ sɔ́tsɛ̀n wù bí? tà àndɔ́ mɔ̀nljú?ɔ́ kɔ́ dí? lɔ̀ vèwê à kùɔ́ ŋgɔ́? à wù.' àndɔ́ yɔ́ gá?ɔ̀ lì yɔ̀ɔ́ mɔ́, wàjn jí mɔ́, tì?ɔ́ wénɔ́ mɔ́ sɔ́ kí lá yɔ̀ɔ́ ʒʉ́ lí kɔ̀ɲʉ̀ á yɔ́ gá?ɔ̀. yɔ̀ɔ́ sɔ́ lù nɔ́?ɔ́ ɔ̀ʒʉ̀ ɔ̀ kɔ̀ yɔ̀ɔ́ mbɔ́ŋsɔ́ ndʒʉ́ á ɔ́kù ɔ́ ndʒé?ɔ́ tsú?, ŋkɔ́ŋ kɔ̀ntsù? ŋkɔ́ŋ kɔ̀ntsù? ŋkɔ́ŋ kɔ̀ntsù?, ɔ́ nví ŋkám ŋkámɔ́ ŋkám kɔ́ nlwín á dʒɔ́kɔ́ mpfén yɔ̀ɔ́ mɔ́ ndʒʉ́ ntɔ́m á kɔ̀ʃí jí á mɔ̀bí? mjì nɔ́ nvì bí?ɔ́, ŋwú?mɔ́ tsú ʒʉ̀tɔ̀ lì. mɔ́ nljí ndzáŋ jì mɔ́ mbí?.
  ndéléndélé mō wâ
  kùm àfwín fɔ́ tàs
  jɛ̀ lɔ̀ lù fá ŋgwʉ̀?
  kùm àfwín fɔ́ ʒʉ̀?
  ndélé mō wâ
  ndéléndélé mō wâ
mɔ̀kúm mjì, mɔ̀bí? mjìmɔ́ mbɛ́ nʒá?ɔ́ mfʉ́ fá ɔ́kù jì ɔ́bén ɔ́bén ɔ́bén ɔ̀ sɔ́tsɛ̀n vɔ̀wenɔ́ mbwá?kɔ́ nɔ́?ɔ́ ɔ̀ʒʉ̀ ɔ̀ kɔ̀ mɔ́ nlú ndʒʉ́ á kɔ̀ʃí á vɔ̀wenɔ́ nɔ́ ndʒʉ̀ɔ̀ ŋwú? tsú. yɔ̀ɔ́ nljí dʒɔ́kɔ̀ kɔ̀ntsù? jì nví ntɔ́m lúwɛ̀n. wì? á yɔ̀ nɔ́ mmwɔ̀mɔ̀ yɔ̀ɔ́ mwɔ́m á mbì ŋgá?á 'ɔ́? ɔ̀? ɔ̀? à dì? kɔ̀ntsù? à dì? kɔ̀ntsù?'. vɔ̀wenɔ́ mmwɔ́m tá lì ŋgá? tá lì nɔ́?ɔ́ vɔ̀tsɛ̀m 'ɔ́? ɔ̀? ɔ̀? à dì? kɔ̀ntsù? à dì? kɔ̀ntsù?'. vɔ̀wenɔ́ , vɔ̀wenɔ́ mɔ́ ŋyá? wájn jì lúwɛ̀n ŋkɔ́ŋ mɔ́ŋ lúwén nláŋ, nɔ́?ɔ̀ kɔ̀ʃí kɔ̀ kɔ̀ á kɔ́ dí?ɔ̀ à wén ɔ́wɛ̀n á kɔ́ kú ɔ́fwɔ́f vɔ́ nláŋsɔ́ nɔ́?ɔ́ ɔ̀ʃì ɔ̀tsɛ̀m nláŋsɔ́ ɔ́tí?ɔ́tí?ɔ́ wén, nláŋsɔ́ áʃíɔ́ wén, nláŋsɔ́ álwíɔ́ wén mɔ́ mfʉ́ nɔ̀ wén ɔ́ ŋwú á ndʒɔ́ á ɔ̀tʃʉ̀ɔ́ ŋgɔ́ŋ á lɔ̀ fá kɔ́bɔ́ŋ. àndɔ́ vɔ́ wʉ́ɔ̀ lì wàjn jí mɔ́ sɔ́ dí? á kɔ̀ʃí jì. tì?ɔ́ wénɔ́ sɔ́ vì mú?ɔ́ yɔ̀ sɔ̀ bɔ́?sɔ́ á mɔ́pfʉ́. tì?ɔ́ wénɔ́ nsáj nɔ́?ɔ́ ɔ̀ʒʉ̀ ɔ̀ kɔ̀ njén wájn jì yɔ̀ dí? á kɔ̀ʃí jì yɔ̀ɔ́ nljí kɔ̀ɲíŋ ɔ́ nví nljí wén nɔ́?ɔ́ ɔ̀ʒʉ̀ ɔ̀ kɔ̀

114

mbá?tā əfó vjí fá wɛ́nə́ ʃí ə́wɛ̀n á vɔ́ jì làŋsə́ lì. àndə́ ɣə́ bá?tə̀ lì ŋkwɛ́n á ə́kù tà nə̀ ŋàŋŋàŋ nʃə́tə́ áljù?. mú?ə́ ɣə̀, tà àndə́ ɣə́ bá?tə̀ lì mə́ mbə́mtə́ à wàjn ji lá à jì tʃò ɣɔ̀ lɔ́. wàjn ji mə́ nʃə́?tə́ á wɛ́n. ɣə̀ə́ ŋkwɛ́n á ə́kù tà nə̀ ŋàŋŋàŋ nʃə́tə́ áljù? jí mfʉ́. mbí?ə́ ndzáŋ jí mbí?ə́ mbí?ə́ mbí? və̀wenə́ , mə̀bí? mjìmə́ ntsɛ́ntā mbɛ́n lúwɛ̀n vɔ́ ndʒʉ́ ŋkwɛ́n nzí á mə́ɲʉ́ nɔ́?ə́ ə̀ʒʉ̀ ə̀ kɔ̀ bà?ə́ jí mfʉ́ á kə́bə́ŋ nljí gə̀ ɲíŋsə́ ntɔ́m á ə̀tʃʉ̀ ŋgə̀ŋ ntʃwánə́ mbvà? ə́ mɔ́? tsú mə̀bí? mjìmə́ mfwí.

ŋgàjnə́ mə́ mmé á kə̀ʃí á jɛ̀n. pfə̀pfə̀pfə̀, wù bwí wàjnə́ wù ɣə̀ə́ ŋkú?ə́ tá bwàbwà? ŋkà wù kú?ə́ tá bwàbwà?.

The Stubborn Child and the Ungrateful Monkeys
Once upon a time a man had a son. The man will go and tap palmwine, bring to his home and then play his xylophone for monkeys to come out of the forest and dance. After dancing he will offer them the palmwine as entertainment. The monkeys will drink the palmwine and then return to the forest. The child always watched with interest and admiration.

One day his father was leaving home and the child told him that during the day he will play the xylophone for the monkeys to come and dance. The father refused telling him that if he dares, the monkeys will trouble him since he will not have palmwine to entertain them with. The man then left thinking that the child had understood and will obey him.

However when the man was gone the child went to the palm bush to harvest the forest sour fruit. He came home, squeezed the juice and put into jugs as if it were palmwine. After that he started to play the xylophone just like his father. The monkeys came out in their numbers and danced as usual. When they were exhausted they went in and sat as they always do and the boy brought them the jugs. The monkey that always tasted their wine tasted and wondered what type of palmwine it was. Each of them tasted and said that it was wine from the forest sour fruit not palmwine. Because this annoyed them they

tied up the child and closed all openings on his body such that no air went in or out of him. They kept him at the entrance to the house and left. The child nearly died but his father arrived on time to save him. After rescuing the child he explained to his father what had happened so he quickly rushed to the palm bush and tapped palmwine. He returned and started to play the xylophone for the monkeys to come and dance. As usual they came out in their numbers and danced until they got tired. They then went in to sit and drink. While they were drinking the man carried a large bundle of grass, placed on the door and set fire on it. All the monkeys got burnt and died.
    This is the end of the story.

5) Wùwì nə̀ ə̀fú ə́ fə́kɔ̀ʔ
Narrator: ntìə́
Audience: mbòó
Narrator: wù ŋgwʉ̀ʔ nə̀ nlʉ̆ ló
Audience: ò
Narrator: ə̀ tʃʉ́ʔə́ nlájn ɣə̀ə́ nlú ndʒʉ́ á bwí ŋkɔ́ʔ ló
Audience: ə̀ŋ
Narrator: ɣə̀ə́ ndʒʉ́ ŋkwέn á ə̀kù ə́ sə́ bwí ŋkɔ́ʔ bwí ŋkɔ́ʔ sə́tsὲn ə̀fú ə̀ fə̀kɔ̀ʔ ə̀ ntánə́ nʃíʔə́ ŋɣáŋtə́ á wέnə́ dzə́m. ɣə̀ə́ mbwí ŋkɔ́ʔ mjì mmé mə́ ŋgáʔ lá ɣə̀ ʃíʔə́ fà jí dzə́m jì kúʔsə́ ŋkɔ́ʔ mjì. ɣə̀ə́ ŋgáʔə́ ɣə̀á kúʔsə́ tà nə̀ jì á dzə́m. ɣə̀ə́ ŋkúʔsə́ ŋkɔ́ʔ mjìmə́ mmé nlú lúwὲn ndʒʉ̀ə̀ ndʒʉ̀ə̀ ŋkwέn á ŋgə̀ŋ. ŋgáʔə́ ɣə̀ ʃíʔə́ fà jí dzə́m jì ʃíʔsə́ ŋkɔ́ʔ mjì fá wέnə́ kə̀tʃú. ŋgáʔə́ ɣə̀á ʃíʔsə́ tà nə̀ wέná dzə́m. ɣə̀ə́ nʃíʔsə́ ŋkɔ́ʔ mjìmə́. mbέ ŋgáʔə́ 'ʃíʔə́ fà mò ə́ dzə́m mà kwέn á ŋgə̀ŋ.' ɣə̀ə́ ŋgáʔá 'wù á kwέn tà nə̀ mò á dzə́m.' ɣə̀ə́ kwέn lí mmé á ŋgə̀ŋ lúwὲn kə̀ɲù kjí mə̀ sə́ kú ŋgə́ʔ á wέn lá jìə̀ lá ŋwúʔ ə̀fú ə́ fə̀kɔ̀ʔə́ díʔ à jí dzə́m á lέ ló. kə́ ntʃó wέn lúwὲn ɣə̀ə́ mə́ ŋkə́ŋə́ ŋkáŋ mpfέ mə́ sə́ làʔtə̀ ŋkáŋ jì lúwέn lóə́, làʔtə̀ mwɔ́mə̀ làʔtə̀ mwɔ́mə̀. ndʒə̀ jì, ɣə̀ə́ lì mwɔ́mə̀ á lì mə́ bwɔ́msə̀ lá ɣə̀ fwɔ́mə́ nóʔə̀ nàntô. ə̀fú ə̀ fə̀kɔ̀ʔ jí mə́ nsìə́ nʃíʔə́ fá wέnə́

dzə́m lúwèn. mə̀ nzìə́ sə́ là?tə̀ ŋkáŋ jì tjú lóə́ là?tə̀ lóə́. ɣə̀ə́ mə́ ɲíŋ lúwèn mfʉ́ ndʒʉ́ nljə́mtə́. ə̀ ə̀fʉ́ ə̀ fə̀kɔ̀? jí mjétə́ ŋkáŋ jì mbɛ́ nlú lúwèn ŋkə́ŋə́ ntʃɨm mə́ sə́ bɨ́?tə́ dʒʉ̀ə̀
    wù ŋgwʉ̀? nə̀ nlɔ̀ptə́ mɔ̀ə́
    ljɨm ntswɔ́ŋ
    wù ŋgwʉ̀? nə̀ nlɔ̀ptə́ mɔ̀ə́
    ljɨm ntswɔ́ŋ
    pfè lì fə̀mbù? fə́ ŋkáŋ
    ljɨm ntswɔ́ŋ
wì? jí nʒʉ́ ndzàŋ jì ɣə̀ə́ ɔ́vá mbɔ́ŋ á wɛ́n ɣə̀ə́ mbɛ́ nlú sə́ bɛ́nə́ vì bɛ́ bɛ́nə́ vì. ɣə̀ə́ njɛ́nə́ wɛ́n nɔ́?ə̀ ə̀ʒʉ̀ ə̀ kɔ̀ mə́ mbɛ́ ɲíŋə́ ndʒʉ́ ŋɣáŋtə́ á wɛ́nə́ dzə́m. ɣə̀ə́ mə́ nsɛ́ nə̀ ə̀fʉ́ ə́ fə̀kɔ̀? jí á wɛ́nə́ dzə́m.

ŋgàjnə́ mmɛ́ á kə̀ʃí á jèn. pfə̀pfə̀pfə̀, bwí wàjnə̀ wù ɣə̀ə́ ŋkú?ə́ tá bwàbwà? ŋkà wù bɛ́ kú?ə́ tá bwàbwà?.

The Woman and the Leaf
Once upon a time a woman went to fetch firewood. While she was busy fetching the firewood a leaf came down from a tree and hung on her back. When she had finished she told the leaf to descend from her back so that she could be able to put the firewood on her head. The leaf refused and told her to carry the firewood with it on her back. For that reason the woman tried and took up the wood to her head and walked home. When they arrived she told the leaf to descend so that she could put down the firewood from her head. The leaf said she should go ahead and put down the firewood from her head with it on her back. She put down the firewood and then told the leaf to go down so that she could enter the house. The leaf again said she will only go in with it on her back. Then she went into the house and was troubled wondering how she will sit with a leaf on her back. Finally she decided to look for corn and prepare cornbeer.

When the cornbeer was ready she began to lick it while appreciating how nice it was. The leaf was tempted to taste so it went down from the woman's back and joined her in drinking the cornbeer. As the leaf concentrated on the cornbeer the woman escaped and hid herself outside.

When the leaf had finished licking the cornbeer it went out, looked for a drum and was playing:
    A woman deceived my ... very sweet
    A woman deceived my ... very sweet
    Cooked a pot of cornbeer ... very sweet
    Cooked a pot of cornbeer ... very sweet
The woman heard the song and it pleased her so much that she got out of her hiding and began to dance. When the leaf saw her it flew and landed on her back again and she remained with it.

    This is the end of the story.

B) ŋgàjnsɔ́ 'Riddles'

1) **Tester**: *mó ŋgáí*
Respondants: *ʃiŋ ŋgáí*
Tester: *tə́m ə́ yɔ́ŋ á kə̀ʃí ə̀ tsù? á kə̀dʒʉ́?* 'Shoot a spear someone and remove a heap.'
Response: *à dì? bélə̀ŋ* 'It is groundnut.'
Brief Explanation: A single groundnut seed is planted but a lot of them are found when uprooted during harvest.

2) **Tester**: *mó ŋgáí*
Respondants: *ʃiŋ ŋgáí*
Tester: *lù kə̀ndàŋ ə̀ dʒù ə̀ fáŋ* 'Go for a trip and not return.'
Response: *ə̀fʉ́ ɔ́ fə̀kɔ̀?* 'leaf'
Brief Explanation: A leaf falls from a branch and never goes back to where it was.

3) **Tester**: *mó ŋgáí*
Respondants: *ʃìŋ ŋgáí*
Tester: *ndzáŋ á və́ mɔ́ʔə́ á dʒì və́ mbúʔ tà və̀tsɛ̀m* 'wood xylophone placed on a road and everyone plays'
Response: *ə̀lò* 'bridge'
Brief Explanation: The local xylophone is made up of pieces of wood line together in a similar manner like the local bridges are constructed. When a bridge has been made like the xylophone, everyone has the freedom to use the bridge to cross the water.

4) **Tester**: *mó ŋgáí*
Respondants: *ʃìŋ ŋgáí*
Tester: *ljə́ŋ ə̀bùʔ ə̀wúm ə̀ jèn wùwí ə́ ntúʔ* 'Go through ten doors and see a palace woman (Fon's wife).'
Response: *à dìʔ ə̀sáŋ* 'It is corn.'
Brief Explanation: Before one sees the corn on the cob one has to remove the leaves from the whole maize. removing the leaves is similar to penetrating the palace in order to see the Fon's wife who normally stays in or around the palace and does not move around freely so that she is rarely seen.

5) **Tester**: *mó ŋgáí*
Respondants: *ʃìŋ ŋgáí*
Tester: *bwí fá ɲì ə̀ kə̀wù̀* 'give birth through a toe'
Response: *kə̀ntsùʔ* 'forest sour fruit'
Brief Explanation: Normally trees produce fruit through the branches, trunck, or stems but this tree rather produces at the base. The others that produce elsewhere are considered to behave like a woman who gives birth through her vigina which is located below the waist but this one that produces fruit at the base is considered to be a woman who rather gives birth through her toe.

6) **Tester**: *mó ŋgáí*
Respondants: *ʃìŋ ŋgáí*
Tester: *làm mànàŋ á kàtʃʉ́ ə́ mpfí* 'plan evil on a mother's head'
Response: *əkú* 'forest'
Tester: *ə́ʔ ə̀* 'no'
Response: *əkjéʔ* 'tray'
Tester: *ə́ʔ ə̀* 'no'
Response: *á kó díʔ əsáŋ* 'Isn't it corn?'
Tester: *ə́ʔ ə̀* 'no'.
 yə̀ŋ kú fɔ̀jn à mò mà ʃə́ʔtə́ à yə̀ŋ 'Give me a Fon let me tell you the answer'
Respondants: *jènə́ kú lí fɔ̀jn kɔ̀m à wù* 'We give you the Fon of Kom'
Tester: *sɨ́ʔ fɔ̀jn kɔ̀m tʃò vì júwù ŋwʉ́ʔmə́ à ʃə̀ ə́ nsáŋlə̀* 'Great Fon of Kom, come over let us sit here and be rejoicing'.
 à dìʔ kə̀làŋ á wú ljɨ́ə́ tùtù ə́ nʒɨ́ tsú. 'It is achu (pounded cocoyams) which you eat with cocoyam leaves soup.'
Brief Explanation: Cocoyams produce the leaves so if one takes makes achu from cocoyams and turns around to use the leaves as soup for eating the achu from cocoyams it is as if a child plans evil for its mother.

Tester: *mó ŋgáí*
Respondants: *ʃìŋ ŋgáí*
Tester: *lù wàjn ə̀ bjèʔə̀ mpfí* 'A child gets up and carries its mother.'
Response: *ŋgùʔə̀ bjɨ* 'camwood grinding stone'
Brief Explanation: The small stone used in grinding (camwood) on the big stone sits on it as expected but it puts

pressure on it as it grinds substances whereas it is unusual for a child to put pressure on the mother.

8) **Tester:** *mó ŋgáí*
Respondants: *ʃìŋ ŋgáí*
Tester: *ɲàm ə̀ ndɔ́ŋ mù?* 'a one horn cattle'
Response: *kə̀pfɨ́sə́* 'umbrella'
Brief Explanation: An umbrella has one handle that looks like the horns of cattle. However cattle have two horns but the umbrella has only one.

9) **Tester:** *mó ŋgáí*
Respondants: *ʃìŋ ŋgáí*
Tester: *ə̀kásə́ ʃɨ ə̀ kjìʔə́ ntú?* 'worn-out hoes of palace women'
Response: *àwʉ́ ə́ mbvʉ́sə̄* 'chickens' feet'
Brief Explanation: Chickens normally walk bare-footed all the time and so their feet are supposed to be worn-out just like the old hoes that have been used by palace women for long periods of time.

10) **Tester:** *mó ŋgáí*
Respondants: *ʃìŋ ŋgáí*
Tester: *ɲì ŋgwòlə́ŋ* 'sharp machete'
Response: *kə̀záŋ ká àljù?* 'palm frond'
Brief Explanation: A palm frond like a sharp machete can cut up a person's body if handled carelessly.

C) tə̀gà? tə̀ tótə́ 'Proverbs'

1) *ə̀ŋgɔ̀m ə́ wùdʒìŋ ə́ kó nə́ ntó á kə́tsàŋ* 'A hungry person's banana/plantain does not grow to maturity.'

Explanation: *à dǐʔ bjì fámbúm á è, à dìʔ lá wìʔ nə́ nljɨ̀ə̀ wàjn ə̀ wέn tà bwáʔ kó ndǐʔ á ɣə̀ tɨ́mə̀ tò á wùwì ɣə̀ə́ mə̀ kù á ə́lám. kə̀á kə́ bɔ́ŋə́ lí. kə̀á kə́ bɔ́ŋə́ lí. kə́ dǐʔ lá və́ɣə́n ə́ ŋwɨ́ vɨ́ndʒə́ sə́tsὲn wìʔ tó ə̀kwὺʔ á wùwì ə̀kɨ́ kə̀ɲὺ və́ mə̀ kùə́ wέn á ŋgə̀ŋə́ ə́lám.* 'This is because people sometimes take their immature daughters and send to marriage. It is not nice and it is better that we should allow our children to mature and be ready for marriage before we give them out.'

2) *fə̀kɔ̀ʔ fə́ wùlwìn fə́ nə́ ŋkwàʔə̀ tà ə̀fwɔ́f* 'An honest man's tree is usually broken only by wind.'

Explanation: *kə́ dǐʔ lá wù nə́ ndǐʔ ə̀ʒɨ́ tséɣə́ wù ŋwɨ́ʔ wùə́ kó kɨ́ə́ tě wù á kjǐʔə̀ kə̀fó. wùə́ nə̀ sə́ kɨ̀plə̀ tà álə̀ ɲìŋgɔ̀ŋ gjámtə́ wìʔə̀ kù kə̀fó à wù.* 'This is said because a good, honest person may not be expecting to receive anything and suddenly God directs someone to come and offer them a gift. As such the honest person does not lack unlike a greedy one who can rather face misfortunes. '

3) *là á kə́ màə́ ŋkjǐʔ kə̀mfò bé ɲὺʔə̀ kə̀vú á tfɨ́* 'Let me not have a means to move fire and still burn my hand.'

Explanation: *kə́ dǐʔ lá sə́tsὲn mà kjǐʔə̀ ə́fèʔ vɨ́nə́ dǐʔə́ gjàmtə́ mó wìʔə̀ kó dǐʔə́ gjàmtə́.* 'This can be said by a parent who has some work to do and expects children (who are supposed to help their parents) to help out but they do not.'

4) *kɜvú kɜmùʔ kɔ́ kó zì kɜ̀ kwíʔɜ́ ɜ̀bíʔ* 'One hand cannot tie a bundle.'

Explanation: *à dìʔ lá sɔ́tsèn víʔɜ́ ndíʔ á ŋgɜ̀ŋ vɜ́ ntsɛ̀ntɜ̀ ʃèʔɜ̀ á kɜ̀ɲù̵ lá kɜ̀mùʔ.* 'This means that if people are together they should cooperate and work as one.'

5) *tó tó á wándʒɜ̀ ɜ̀ jɛ̀nɜ́ mbjí* 'Child, grow up and see life.'

Explanation: *kɔ́ díʔ lá vú̵ndʒɔ́ ɔ́ lù̵ tà vɜ̀tʃétɜ́ vɜ́ sɜ́ kɔ́ŋɜ́ ɜ̀ nè ɜ̀ɲù̵ á wìʔɔ́ kó díʔ ébɜ̀ ɜ́nè.* 'This is said because some young people try to do things that are not within their reach.'

6) *lá fɜ̀ɲín fɔ́ gáʔɜ̀ ɜ̀tʃù̵ fɔ́ kó nɜ́ nʃèʔɜ̀ ɜ̀lɔ̀ʔ* 'A bird that only makes noise cannot build a nest.'

Explanation: *à dìʔ bjìʔɜ̀ wìʔ á yɔ́ gàʔɜ̀ tà ɜ̀tʃù̵ yɜ́ɜ́ kó nè tè kɜ̀ɲù̵ kɜ̀tsén; tà ʒíkɜ́dʒàŋ.* 'This is because of a lazy person who just makes plans but never realize them.'

7) *vɜ́ gàʔɜ̀ lá wìʔ ʒí á ljìmɜ̀ yɜ̀ gàʔɜ̀ lá jì á ʒí á ɜ̀fú̵* 'They say that a person should eat in a plate but he says he will eat in a leaf.'

Explanation: *á kɔ́ mínsɔ́ lá ɜ̀ vɜ́ jɛ́nɜ́ kɜ̀ɲù̵ kɜ̀ tímɜ́ kɔ́ á lɜ̀ gàʔɜ̀ lá wù̵ né kɜ̀ɲù̵ kɜ̀ tímɜ́ wù̵ gàʔɜ̀ lá wù̵ á nè tà kjìkɔ́ á kɔ́ bɔ́ŋɜ̀ à wù̵. wù̵ né á lì à né ndíʔ áftà kó ndíʔ á kɔ́á fù̵ á dʒí.* 'It talks about someone who is stubborn and even though they tell him what is right he insists on doing just that which he prefers but eventually fails.'

8) *lá wìʔə́ kə́ŋə́ tímə́ á nsé ə́fɨ̀lə̀ ə́ ŋgə̀ŋ* 'A person wants to stand on the ground and roof a house.'

Explanation: *kə́ mìnsə̀ lá wìʔə́ kə́ŋə́, lá wù kə́ŋə́ nè kə̀nɨ̀ á wù kó tímə̀ kwɨ̀ʔə́ nè.* 'It is said to a person who is too ambitious, trying to do only things they are not yet able to do.'

9) *və́ nə́ ndʒèʔə̀ nə̀ wàjn á dzέm kó ɣə̀ə́ kɨ́ lá kə̀ɣáf kə́ dʒì kə́ dʒə̀fə̀* 'When a child goes on the back it doesn't know that the distance is long?'

Explanation: à díʔ múʔə́ kə́ mìnnə́ lá tàndə́ wú díʔə̀ və́ kú ə̀fó tà kúə́ à wù, wù tsὲnə̀, wù káʔsə́ tsὲnə̀ kə̀fó tà tsὲnə̀ wùə́ kó kɨ́ə́ lá kə́ lù fá fέnə́ lɔ́. wùə́ sə́ né nɔ́ʔə̀ ɣə̀ tsú á wù kwòʔtə̀.* 'It is said about someone who only receives things without working and as such is not careful with what they receive and just squanders or misuses the thing.'

10) *kə́á jέnə́ ə̀kú fá mə̀fέn* 'Do not value a forest from its darkness.'

Explanation: *ə́ jέn wíʔá lə̀ á dʒì múʔə́ mə́ díʔ múʔə́ ɣə́ fɨ́ə̀ lí nɔ́ʔə́ lə̀ wù múʔə́ ŋkwòʔə̀ lá ɣə̀ dìʔ á lə̀ kɨ́ʔ kə̀fó á kə̀vú ŏ ɣə̀ zí ɣə̀ né tὲ kə̀nɨ̀ á kə́ fɨ́ á dʒì kó ndíʔ á ɣə̀ á nè ə́ kə́ fɨ́ á dʒì.* 'It warns that appearance is not reality such that you shouldn't see someone who is well dressed and then think that the person has money or that the person can do something worthy whereas he doesn't have nor can do anything impressive.'

D) mɜ̀tǐtì bjì ɜ̀ɲʉ̀ 'Myths about realities'

1) bùʃí wɛ́nɜ̀ tʃŏkwʉ̀ʔ 'Cat and rat'

mà kɜ́ŋɜ́ ʃɜ̀ʔtɜ̀ kɜ̀ɲʉ́ á kɔ́ nè lá bùʃí njɛ́nɜ́ tʃŏkwʉ̀ʔ nɔ́ʔɜ̀ fɛ́nɜ́ ɣɜ̀ɜ́ sɜ́ dzɨ̀mɜ̀ tá jì á ɣá ʔɜ́ pfɨ́ʔ. à ndɨ̀ʔ nɔ́ʔɜ́ támɜ̀ mbì, bùʃí wɛ́nɜ́ tʃókwʉ̀ʔ ndɨ̀ʔ ndôŋ, nɔ́ʔɜ̀ ndôŋ ɜ́tó. ɜ̀tʃʉ́ʔ nlájn kɜ́tsí kɜ̀tsɛ́nkɔ́ vɜ̀wé nlú sɜ́ dʒɛ̀ʔɜ̀ ɣántɜ̀, ŋɣántɜ́ ŋɣántɜ́ ŋɣántɜ́, ndjʉ̀ nzáʔá á kɜ́ʃí kɜ́tsɛ́nkɔ́ ɜ̀wʉ́ tsɛ́ɣɜ́ nʃǐʔɜ́, ɜ̀wʉ́ nví álɜ̀ nví nví nví. vɜ̀wé, nné ntʃó, vɜ̀wé bwínɜ́ á mɜ́pfwô, ɜ́ sɜ́ djʉ̀ ɜ́záʔá á fwànɜ́ mùɜ̀ múʔɜ́ múɜ̄ lwín lí bjì ɜ̀wʉ́ jí á ɣɜ̀ jì vì nántó lì. vɜ̀wé mjɔ́ʔsɜ́ dʒí á vɔ́ á tím, mjɔ́ʔsɜ́, kɜ̀ɲʉ́ kjíkɜ́ mɜ̀ tʃò bùʃí bjɛ́ʔɛ́ bùʃí kó nɜ́ ŋkù ɜ́ kùmsɜ́ múɜ̄ bwɛ́n. bùʃí, tʃŏkwʉ̀ʔ ntsɔ́ʔ á tʃì à mùɜ̀ nsám nsám nsám ndjʉ̀ nzáʔá á ʃɜ̀ á là, á kɜ̀ntìntìn ɜ́ njén lá jì zì jì tím, ɜ́ bwínɜ́ nví ŋgáʔ à bùʃí lá: áìj, jì zì jì májnsɜ́ ɜ̀tím. bùʃí nsɛ́nsɜ́ wɛ́n lá ɣɜ̀ tsɔ́ʔsɜ́ jí, ɣɜ̀ bjɛ́ʔɛ́ jí ló ɜ̀tím ɜ̀ wʉ́ jí ɜ̀ndɜ́ ɣɜ̀ jɛ́n lí lá jì zì jì tím lì. ɜ̀m, tʃŏkwʉ̀ʔ, tʃŏkwʉ̀ʔ ntʃɛ́n lá bùʃí sɜ̀ kɜ́ŋɜ́ dʒì lá jì bjɛ́ʔɛ́ jí ló wɛ́nɜ́ wɛ́n ljɜ́ŋ ɜ̀ndɜ́ bùʃí ɔ̀và ɣɔ́ʔɜ́. tʃŏkwʉ̀ʔ ntʃɛ́n, nʃwáŋɜ́ wɛ́n á tʃì à mùɜ̀ ɜ́ nsámɜ́ ntím. bùʃí ntímɜ́ á kɜ́ʃí jì ŋkwɔ́ʔ kɜ̀ɲʉ̀ á ɣɜ̀ á nè, ŋkwɔ́ʔ ŋkwɔ́ʔ ɣɜ̀ɜ́ kó kɨ́. kɜ̀ɲʉ̀ kjí nzáfɜ́ wɛ́n á lɜ̀ lá wùndɔ́ŋɜ̀ jí tʃŏkwʉ̀ʔ mɜ̀ kjè jí álɜ̀ lɔ́. ɣɜ̀ɜ́ nlú ndʒɛ́ʔtɜ́ nʃǐʔí ndjʉ́ fá ɜ́ʃɜ́ á là nʃǐʔí ndjʉ́ lá jì á jén kɜ́ʃí ʃwàŋ fá tsú tím ɣɜ̀ɜ́ kó jén. mbwìnɜ́ ŋkúʔ fá ɜ́ʃɜ́ á là ŋkɔ́ŋ ŋkɔ́ŋ ŋkɔ́ŋ sɜ́tsɛ̀n ɣɜ̀ɜ́ njɛ́n fɜ́ʃínɜ́ fɜ́tsɛ́nfɜ́ á ɣɜ́ zì ɣɜ̀ ʃwáŋ. ɣɜ̀ nʃwáŋ ɜ̀tìm. ɣɜ̀ɜ́ sɜ́ djʉ̀ ɜ́ mɜ̀ njɛ́n, ɣɜ̀ɜ́ sɜ́ pfwó ɜ́ mɜ̀ njɛ́n tʃŏkwʉ̀ʔ, múʔɜ́ tʃŏkwʉ̀ʔ ɜ́ mɜ́ pfwǒ sɜ́ zɔ́jtɜ́ ɜ́ʒíʔ, mɜ́ zɔ́jtɜ́ mɜ́ wʉ́ lá bùʃí lɜ́ né sè á kɜ́ʃí jì ò. bùʃí nʃwáŋ á tjínɜ́ fwí lá jì kɜ́ŋɜ́ ɣáʔ wɛ́n ɜ́ ɣɔ̀m nɔ́ʔɜ́ ɣómɜ́. ɣɜ̀ɜ́ ɲíŋ ɜ́ ŋkwɛ́n á tʃì kɜ̀bɨ̀ʔ. bùʃí mɜ́ ŋgáʔ á wɛ́n lá ɜ̀ndɜ́ ɣɜ́ ɲíŋɜ́ ŋkwɛ́n á tʃì kɜ̀bɨ̀ʔ lì ɣɜ̀ sé tà tsú bjɛ́ʔɛ́ nɔ́ʔɜ́ fɛ́nɜ́, nɔ́ʔɜ́ zɛ́nɜ́ á jìɜ́ lú ɣáʔɜ́ wɛ́n, jì á ɣáʔɜ́ wɛ́n ɜ́ pfɨ́ʔ tà pfɨ́ʔɜ́. fá zɔ́jn ájì ɜ́ záʔá fá

125

lájn bùʃí mɔ́ sɔ́ dʒɛ̀ʔɛ̀ nɔ́ʔɔ̀ fɛ́nɔ̀ á ɣɔ̀ jɛ́nɔ̀ tʃŏkwʉ̀ʔ, ɣɔ̀ dzɨ̀mtɔ̀ tà dzímtɔ̀ lá jì á ɣáʔ.

Cat and Rat

I want to tell you why the cat chases the rat to catch and eat everywhere they meet. In the past Cat and Rat were very close friends. One day they went out visiting and it happened that rain met them and fell heavily. They took shelter somewhere and after the rain they started home. They came to a stream that was inundated following the heavy rain. They stood there and began to wonder how they would cross, especially because Cat doesn't like water. Rat dived inside and swam to a distance and returned to tell Cat they he could cross. Cat begged Rat to carry him across since Rat could swim. Rat refused saying that Cat was too heavy and they could drown if he (Rat) carried him (Cat). Rat then dived into the water and swam across leaving Cat behind. Cat was really disappointed and shocked that his friend abandoned him. Cat moved downwards along the stream but never found a place to cross throw. He then move upwards and finally he found a narrow area over which he could skip over to the other side. Rat had been keeping himself warm around a fire at home and imagining that Cat could never cross the stream. When Cat arrived, with all the anger he wanted to catch Rat and beat him up but Rat escaped and entered into a hole. Cat then told him to not show up any more because if ever they met he will catch Rat and eat. Ever since Cat has been chasing Rat each time they see each other.

2) dzɛ̀mɔ̀ tɔ̀lɔ̀kjí

Mɔ̀ɲín ɔ̀ ŋkjìʔ mítì á ɔ̀kàŋ. Wù kɔ́ŋɔ́ ʃɔ̀ʔtɔ̀ kɔ̀ɲʉ̀ á kɔ́ nê dzɛ̀mɔ̀ tɔ̀lɔ̀kjí... kɔ̀ɲʉ̀ á kɔ́ nê dzɛ̀mɔ̀ tɔ̀lɔ̀kjí sɔ́ díʔ á ŋgwóʔsɔ́ á ŋgwóʔsɔ́. fámbú á vɔ̀wé...ɣɔ̀ njɛ́n mɔ́ɲín, mɔ̀ɲín mɔ́ díʔ?

nɔ́ʔə̀...bjɛ́ʔɛ́ yə̀ ndì? nɔ́ʔə̀ ndôŋ nɔ́ʔə̀ nə̀, nɔ́ʔə̀ tɛ̀ kájnə̀ ɲàm kɔ́ à dì? tà wùndɔ́ŋə́ wɛ́n, kɔ̀ dì? tà fə̀ɲín, kɔ́ à dì? ɲàm á yə̀ dʒɛ̀ʔɛ̀ dʒɛ́ʔɛ̀ à dì? tà wùndɔ́ŋə́ wɛ́n, tɛ̀ ʃʉ̀ bjɛ́ʔɛ́ yə́ kwɛ́nə́ á mùə̀ yə̀ə́ bɛ́ sə́ sàmə̀ múə̄ tá nə̀ ʃʉ̀. múʔɔ́ nlɔ́jn və̀wé lá jì kɛ́ dì? víʔə́ ndɔ́ŋsə́ və̀wé á lə̀ və́ djʉ̀ə̀ á mítì bɛ́ dì? kɛ́ və́ dzàŋə̀ jì álɛ́ lɔ́? və̀wɛ́nə́ mə́ ŋkú? á mítì á ə̀kàŋ. mítì mə̀ mə̀ɲìn dí? á ə̀kàŋ? ə̀ŋ. wɛ́nə̀ mə̀ɲín ə́ mə́, mə̀ɲín ə́ mə́,nɔ́ʔə̀ fə̀ɲín fə̀kɔ̀ fə́ mə́ ŋkú ə̀ɲìnə̀, fə̀ɲín fə̀kɔ̀ fə́ sʉ̀ə̀ ə̀ɲìnə̀ á wɛ́nə́ wèn. ə́dʒɔ́jntə́ tə̀vò tə́ ŋkwʉ́? və̀wé mə́ nlú ndjʉ́ á mítì. múʔə́ və́ mə́ jí ŋkú tə̀ʒíʔ? yə̀ə́ mə́ ŋgáʔá ə̀ʒíʔə́ jí díʔ və̀wévə̀tsèm.
ŋkwɛ́n á mítì, fɔ̀jnə́ mə́ nví nə̀ ə̀fóʒívə́ lá à dìʔə̀ ə̀fóʒívə́ yə̀ŋvə̀tsèm. yə̀ə́ mə́ ónnə́ ŋgáʔ lá ə̀ʒíʔə́ jí díʔ yə̀ŋvə̀tsèm. sǒ à dì? tà kákù ə́jí sǒ wìʔə́ kó bɛ́nə́ á kùm. dʒìə́ kó bɛ̀ díʔ ə́ wìʔ bɛ́ sɔ́ʔ. ə̀ŋ dʒìə́ nɔ́ʔə̀, nsɔ́ʔə́ kó díʔ, kɔ́tə́ kó bɛ̀ díʔ. bjɛ̀ʔɛ̀ à dìʔ ə̀ʒíʔə́ wɛ́n. ə̀ŋ.
fə̀ɲín fə́, mə̀ɲín mjìə́ mə́ ŋgáʔ lá lúwèn àndə́ kə́ dìʔ á pòsíʃɔn jèn lɔ́ kə́ dì? lá və̀wé, nɔ́ʔə̀ fə̀ɲín fə́kɔ̀ fə́ nvì tsúʔə́ ə̀ɲìnə̀ ə́ wɛ́n fá wɛ́nə́ ə̀wèn ə̀ jèn dʒí á ŋkà wɛ́nə́ ná pfwó. mə̀ɲín ə́ mə́ nvì ntsúʔtə́ tə̀ɲìnə̀ fá wɛ́nə́ ə̀wèn. nɔ́ʔə̀ fə̀ɲín fə́kɔ̀ fə́ vìə̀ tsúʔə́ mə́ pfwóə́, nɔ́ʔə̀ fə́kɔ̀ fə́ vìə̀ tsúʔə́ mə́ pfwóə́. làs wán á yə́ vì ntsú? yə̀ə́ mə́ nsɛ́nsə́ wɛ́n lá nsɛ́nsɛ́n lɔ́ yə̀ ʃíʔə̀ gàʔ à wìə̀ jí lá yə̀ kə́ŋ və́ dɔ́nlɔ́p ə̀ bàʔtə́ á nsɛ́ à jì bjɛ̀ʔɛ́ jì jɛ́nə́ lá jìə́ né tàn á díʔə̀ nə̀ plèn ə́ mə́ bvɨ̀. wìʔ jí nʃíʔí kə̀ɲʉ́ kə́ ə̀fóʒívə́ kjìkə́ nzáfə́ wɛ́n ə̀ ntʃó, yə̀ ŋgáʔ lá yə̀ tìm ə́tím lá yə̀ wʉ̀ ɲísə́ sə́ ŋkjí tà ə̀káŋ, ə̀ wʉ̀ ndzàmsə́, ə̀ wʉ̀ və́ díkás, ə̀ wʉ̀ áyɔ́ŋ, ə̀ wʉ̀ mbwìsə́ á yə̀ á tàn á nə̀ plèn ə́ bvɨ̀ lɔ́. lùwàjn mə́ mbáʔtə́ ə̀fó mə́ ntím ə́tím lá jí báʔtə́ lí ə̀fó vjɨ̌. yə̀ə́ ntán ə́ mbɔ́ŋsə́ nʃíʔí ŋkwɛ́n á tʃí ndzɔ́ŋsə́. nʃíʔí mbɨpsə́ dzɛ́m ə́ wɛ́n yə̀ə́ sə́ díʔ á bòɲá bòŋ. kə́ kwɛ́ʔə̀ tɔ̀lɔ̀kjí á lì yə̀ tʃìʔí wɛ́n tá kùùù.

Tortoise's broken back
Birds had a meeting. This is to explain why the tortoise has a fragmented back. Birds were to assemble for a meeting in the sky and Tortoise contacted them to ask why they could not

take him along as a friend. Tortoise was indeed a friend to all animals and birds including fish since he can also swim. They accepted to go with him but since the meeting was in the sky and Tortoise could not fly, each bird contributed a feather to build wings for him. When he was ready he took a bird name: Everyone. They flew to the sky for the meeting and after that the king of the birds brought food for entertainment and announced that it was for everyone. Tortoise, now called Everyone, claimed the food since it had been attributed to him. The birds could not say a word since it was logical. However, they got angry and decided to retrieve their feathers from Tortoise. When the last bird came for his feather, Tortoise pleaded with him to tell his wife to place mattrases and place in the yard for him to fly like a plane and land on them. When the bird got home, he told Tortoise's wife, out of anger, that Tortoise said should place machetes, axes, spears and nails to face upward because he will fly and land on them like a plane. This the wife did and then sent word to Tortoise that she was ready. Tortoise then allowed himself to fall down from the sky and when he landed on those objects they destroyed his back. Since he was guilty he keep quiet.

3) Kə̀ɲù á kə́ nèə̀ lá ə̀wú ə́ nvìə̀

Mà kə́ŋə́ bɛ́ ʃə̀ʔtə̀ kə̀ɲù á kə́ nə́ nnè lá ə̀wú nvìə̀. à dì? á lə̀ múʔə́ à ndì? nɔ́ʔə́ mbjì mbì, fòjn ə̀kàŋ wɛ́nə̀ fòjn nsé dí? víʔí ndɔ́ŋsə́. fòjn ə̀kàŋ né nlú mbwí wàjnə̀ wɛ́n yə̀ só lá dzɛ̀ɛ̀ʔ, à mə́ dí? ŋgɛ́sə́ wándʒə̀. wàjnə̀ fòjn nsé dí? tá kə̀ɲàlə̀ á kə̀ɲàlə̀, yə̀ə́ kó bòŋə̀ bwɛ́n. fòjn nsé ŋkwə́? nɔ́ʔə́ kə̀ɲù á yə̀ á nè, ŋkwə́? ŋkwə́? ŋkwə́? ə́ ŋkə̀ŋ dʒí kə̀tsí kə́tsénkə́ ndzáŋ wàjnə̀ fòjn ə̀kàŋ jì lá yə̀ ví yàjntə́ á ntú? ə̀ fòjn nsé. və̀wé né nví nví ŋkwɛ́n, né sə́ ndí? á mə̀djù̀, fòjn nsé ŋkə̀ŋ dʒí ŋkə̀ŋ dʒí və́ nʒwí wàjnə̀ fòjn ə̀kàŋ jì. mbwínə́ ŋkú?, ŋkúʔə́ nʃə́ʔtə́ kə̀ɲù kjíkə́ á fòjn ə̀kàŋ lá kə́ lə̀ dì? á lə̀ múʔə́ wàjnə̀ wɛ́n jì pfú lí. óìj, kə̀ɲù kjíkə́ ŋkwɛ́n á ə̀wɛ́n ə̀ fòjn əkàŋ. kəɲʉ̀ kjíkə́, bjὲʔɛ̀ wàjnə wɛ́n ndì? tà, tà wàjn mú? á lə̀ ɣə̀ só lá dzὲὲ?. fòjn əkàŋ, kəɲʉ̀ kjíkə́ ŋkwɛ́n á wὲn ə̀ fòjn əkàŋ ɣə̀ə́ ndí. àndə́ ɣə́ díə̀ lì mə̀nʃí mə̀ wɛ́n ə́ ntʃɔ́m. mə̀nʃí mə̀ wɛ́n tʃɔ́mə̀ ʃíʔí záʔá nsé à mə́ díʔ ə̀wʉ́ á ɣə́ vìə̀.

ə́ zì fá ə̀tʃʉ́? ájì ə́ záʔá fá lájn sə́tsὲn fòjn əkàŋ ɲʉ́ʔmə́ á lə̀ kwòʔtə̀ bjì wàjnə̀ wɛ́n kwòʔtə̀ kwòʔtə̀ kwòʔtə̀ kwòʔtə̀ ɣə̀ə́ bὲ dì. ɣə̀ dí nɔ́ʔə̀ zɛ́ mə̀nʃí mə̀ wɛ́n ʃíʔí, mə̀ ʃíʔíə̀ à mə́ díʔ ə̀wʉ́ á vɛ́ɣə́ŋ á ʃə̀. sə́tsὲn ɣə̀ bɛ́, kəɲʉ̀ kjí bɛ́ tʃò fá wɛ́nə́ kə̀tʃʉ́ ɣə̀ bɛ́ kjɛ́ ká ɣə̀ bɛ́ná dì, lìmə́ mə̀ bájn. nɔ́ʔə̀ zɛ́ á ɣə́ kwòʔə̀ kwòʔə̀ kwòʔ? ə̀ bὲ zì ə́ dì bjìŋə́ tʃʉ̀ə́, ə̀wʉ́ mə́ sə́ ʃíʔíə̀.

Why it rains
I want to explain why it rains. In the past the King of the sky was a very close friend to the King of the earth. The King of the sky had a very handsome son while that of the earth had an ugly one. Out of jealousy the King of the earth began to think of what to do and someday he invited the son of the King of the sky to come for a visit to the his palace. After spending some time there the child wanted to go back home but the King of the earth plotted and he was killed. They took the news to the King of the sky and the thing pained him so much because that was his only son. In addition he was very handsome. The King of the sky then cried out and shed tears which fell on the earth as rain.

Ever since, each time the King of the sky thinks of his handsome son he cries and his tears pour down to earth as rain. After crying for a while he will stop and forget. Each time he cries we will have much rain which is the rainy season and when he will not be crying there will be no rain and we will have the dry season.

4) ɲàmə̀ tsúʔtə̀ ə̀ɲù
və́ ŋkwèn mítì mə̀ ɲámsə́, ɲámsə́ mə̀ gàʔ lá və́ kə́ kə́ŋ ɲàm á və́ á ntsúʔtə̀ kə̀ɲù̀ tsú. múʔə́ və́ jí ndzàŋ mítì nə́ʔə̀ ɔ́l ɲámsə́, mbvúsə́ ɔ́l. mbvú̀ bə̀ŋsə̀ fáŋ ə̀ sə̀ ʃə̀ʔə̀ tà ə̀ʃí bə́ŋtə́ ə́fó pfíʔtə̀. dén və́ ndjú̀ ŋkwén á mítì nzí fá bjí lá və́ né ntsúʔtə̀, lá və́ á ŋɣáʔə̀ wén tsúʔtə̀ kə̀ɲù̀ tsú. bjí ŋgáʔá dʒɔ̀ʔ, jìə́ kó díʔ á dʒí ájì, ndí á mèè̀ʔ lá jìə́ kó díʔ kájnə̀ wìʔ ájì. néks ɲàm ə̀ ndíʔə́ ŋkwúɲàm múlɔ́ʔ múʔə́ ŋkwúɲàm jì sə́ ntʃə̀ə̀ mbέm á mbvú̀ lá və́ jì dzàŋ mítì ɣə̀ə́ kó djù̀ á mítì álέ lɔ́ʔ mbvú̀ ŋgáʔ á nə́ʔə́ və́ ndjù̀ə̀ tà djú̀ə́ á jí vì. və́ mbέ ŋɣáʔə́ ŋkwúɲàm, ŋkwúɲàm ə́ ŋkúʔsə́ kə̀tʃú̀ kə́ wén nljé ə́ njέn lá mbvú̀ kó jì tímə̀ vì ɣə̀ə́ ŋgáʔ lá nə́ʔə́ à díʔ tà mbvú̀. àndə́ mbvú̀ kó jì vì á mítì lì və́ mə́ ŋkə́nfέmέ tà kə́nfέmέ lá á dìʔ mbvú̀. sə̀̀ dʒìə́ kó dìʔ ə́ və́ fáŋkέ tsúʔtə́ kə̀ɲù̀ tà nə̀ mbvú̀. nə́ʔə̀ fέ á və́ ŋwúʔtə̀, à dìʔ tὲ víʔí və́ ɣáʔə́ tà mbvú̀ ə́tsúʔtə́ kə̀ɲù̀ tsú.

Sacrifice Animal

Once there was a meeting to decide which animal will have to be used for sacrifices. All animals were invited including birds like the chicken. Chicken instead went around looking for things to eat and didn't consider going to the meeting. When Pig was going he asked Chicken why he had not gone for the meeting. Chicken told him to go ahead and he will join them. When they had all gathered and began to discuss, they asked Goat whether they can use him for sacrifices. Goat bleated and said that he is not available. Next they asked Pig whether they could use him. Pig raised his head and looked round but noticed that Chicken was not yet there so he suggested that Chicken should be used. Since Chicken was not present to argue for himself, everyone agreed that he will be the one. Ever since, there is no way any sacrifice can be done without Chicken and each time people gather they use Chicken for their sacrifices.

www.ingramcontent.com/pod-product-compliance
Lightning Source LLC
Chambersburg PA
CBHW061416300426
44114CB00015B/1957